the inflatable
butch

the inflatable
butch

new funny stuff by
ellen orleans

alyson books
los angeles | new york

© 2001 BY ELLEN ORLEANS. ALL RIGHTS RESERVED.

MANUFACTURED IN THE UNITED STATES OF AMERICA.

THIS TRADE PAPERBACK ORIGINAL IS PUBLISHED BY
ALYSON PUBLICATIONS,
P.O. BOX 4371, LOS ANGELES, CA 90078-4371.
DISTRIBUTION IN THE UNITED KINGDOM BY
TURNAROUND PUBLISHER SERVICES LTD.,
UNIT 3, OLYMPIA TRADING ESTATE, COBURG ROAD, WOOD GREEN,
LONDON N22 6TZ ENGLAND.

FIRST EDITION: JULY 2001

01 02 03 04 05 a 10 9 8 7 6 5 4 3 2 1

ISBN 1-55583-569-4

LIBRARY OF CONGRESS CATALOGING-IN-PUBLICATION DATA
ORLEANS, ELLEN, 1961–
   THE INFLATABLE BUTCH : NEW FUNNY STUFF / BY ELLEN
ORLEANS.
   ISBN 1-55583-569-4
   1. LESBIANS—HUMOR. 2. GAY WIT AND HUMOR. I. TITLE.
PN6231.L43 O75 2001
814'.54—DC21   2001022572

COVER DESIGN AND ILLUSTRATION BY PHILIP PIROLO.

For Aunt Jean and Uncle Ron,
who helped foster my independence

Contents

Acknowledgments...ix
Author's Note...xi
Surgeons Made Me Gay!...1
Poly Wants a Lover...5
First-Class Lesbian...9
How to Write a Lesbian Novel...13
Garden-Variety Dykes...17
On the Rocks...20
The Inflatable Butch...27
The Hard, Cold Truth...31
To the Rescue...36
As the Wheels Spin (Part I)...40
As the Wheels Spin (Part II)...45
Whose Cat?...49
The Out Scout...51
Taxes and Gefilte Fish: A Passover Story...57
Sharing the Faith...61
Whatever Gets You Through the Night...67
Cough, Sneeze, Hack, Hack...71

Girlfriend or Vibrator? You Decide!...75
Play With Your Words...78
Go With the (Cash) Flow...87
On the Road—Lesbian Style...92
Sensible Shoes, Practical Pussy...99
Minding Your Matrimonial Manners...103
Barbie, Ben, and Me...107
Here Come the Brides...111
The Lesbian Intervention Squad...114
Bookseller, Bartender, Therapist, Geek...120
Mid-Life at Michigan...124
Steaming...131
What's My Dysfunction?...134
Putting the "Mary" Back in
Merry Christmas...138
Toys Aren't Us...141
Multiple-Choice Madness...145
How's That Again?...150
All Tied Up...154
Poly-Parade Fidelity...158

Acknowledgments

Many thanks to Angela Brown at Alyson Publications for her patience, professionalism, and belief in this book. My appreciation too to Laura Markowitz at *In the Family* for her excellent visioning and revisioning skills. And most of all, thanks to those of you who have offered me unconditional love over the past few years: Alvin, Amanda, Bingo, Charlie, Cleo, Creature, Daisy, Dieter, Dirga, Elsa, Isis, Moriah, Ohksa, Peaches, Pele, Rosie, Ruby, Sadie, Sally, Sappho, Shelly, Star, Texas, Zappa, and Zo. A grateful rub on the tummy to each of you and to your human companions as well.

Author's Note

Many of the essays in *The Inflatable Butch* were published in *Out Front*, *Weird Sisters*, and *In the Family* between 1992 and 1999. They appear here in an order meant to provoke and sustain the largest amount of laughter.

Surgeons Made Me Gay!

Yes, it's true: Traditional Western medicine unleashed my homosexuality. And it's a good thing too, because ever since birth I'd been missing the clues.

Kindergarten, 1966: Seated around a table with four other five-year-olds, I nonchalantly sit in my chair with one leg tucked under the other. Horrified, my teacher hurries toward me and whispers loudly, "That's not ladylike!" I don't know what being a lady has to do with being a five-year-old kid, but this is my first clue that I'm a lesbian. Unfortunately, I miss it completely. I'm too busy learning to tie my shoes.

Fourth Grade, 1971: I'm bitterly disappointed not to be assigned either of the cool fourth-grade teachers, Miss Green or Mr. Hunt, both of whom I later learn are big homos. (Mr. Hunt's platform shoes should have tipped me off.) Instead, I get a new teacher

the inflatable butch

named Miss Feathers. My disappointment turns to fascination when I discover her car in the teachers' parking lot: a forest-green Karmann Ghia with a white convertible top. I fall in love—first with the car, then with her. The quintessential teacher's pet, I am finally rewarded when Miss Feathers invites me to run after-school errands with her, top down.

Two months later, Miss Feathers announces she is getting married. She shows our class the engagement ring. The girls ooh and aah. The boys shrug. I want to throw up.

Sixth Grade, 1973: Donny Solscritch asks me to go steady. I have enjoyed building little villages in the dirt with him during recess, but see no benefits in "being his girl." I know enough to be civil, though, so out of nowhere I pull out an excuse: "My father would object." Donny accepts this and gives me a pressed-flower necklace anyway. At this point, I might have thought of myself as a lesbian, if I'd known what one was.

Seventh Grade, 1974: My older sister gets a copy of *Our Bodies, Ourselves*. First opportunity, I steal it from her bedroom. I read about female sexuality and reproduction, then I get to the chapter, "In Amerika They Call Us Dykes." I read it, then read it again. I'm interested in it from a sociological point of view, I tell myself, not even sure what *sociological* means. During the next five years, I reread that section a dozen times.

Still, I fail to see the big picture. Instead, I'm

the inflatable

butch

busy with lesbian-in-training activities. I swap heterosexual lunchroom socializing for the comforting asexuality of washing test tubes and beakers for my latest role model, Mrs. Richenbacher. To help me with my coming-out process, the Universe sends a slew of dykes and proto-dykes my way: modern, liberated Ms. Deane, yearbook adviser; Miss Brodkin, tough, squat gym teacher for whom I run extra laps; ex-WAC Marge Rogers, the guidance counselor who keeps steering me toward all-girl schools.

College, 1981: I end up at Oberlin, where lesbians are as plentiful as the mung beans I sort during my dining co-op work shift. In fact, four lesbians—hearty members of the Oberlin swim team—are in my co-op. I, however, simply dismiss them as feminists with shaved heads—a hairstyle I'm convinced they've chosen only because it reduces their drag quotient in the water. A freestyler named Randi drops every hint imaginable, yet all I can manage is a friendly, blank stare. Randi and her pals begin a betting pool on when I'll come out. They all lose.

New Jersey, July 1984: Diagnosed with an intestinal malady called Crohn's disease, I am sliced opened. Doctors remove an inflamed portion of my intestine. They blame the disease for my low weight, short stature, and stomach cramps. No one mentions that the affected intestinal section also contained homosexual neutralizing agents. But it must have,

because as I recover I not only develop a taste for tomatoes and green peppers, but also for girls.

Suddenly, life gets a whole lot more interesting.

Poly Wants a Lover

Well, we wouldn't be lesbians if we didn't explore a new sexual slant every few years, and more than that, have a catchy name for it.

Polyamory. It sounds friendly enough. Kind of like Pollyanna. "Oh, honey, it's OK. I see now that you weren't cheating on me. You were just engaging in a little polyamory."

Actually, that's not accurate. One of the givens of a polyamorous relationship is that there's no sneaking around. Extracurricular sex is discussed beforehand, everything out in the open. I only know this because I read it in an article. Truth is, I have no experience in Polyamory Land. OK, once. Sort of.

The year is 1988. I'm 26 years old but have the sexual experience of a houseplant. But that January night, I find myself watching videos at a friend's house, a blanket draped over our laps. Her knee touches

the inflatable butch

mine, but I figure that's because it's a small couch.

The last video ends—it's late—but we begin talking. She explains that she and her lover are trying an "open relationship" for the next few months. For anyone else on the planet, this admission, coupled with the not-so-subtle knee contact, would be an obvious come-on. I, however, assume we are merely having another one of our fascinating interpersonal discussions. Finally, she spells it out for me. She's attracted to me. Am I interested?

I am. I am also nervous. Not to mention inexperienced. *Really* inexperienced. I'm thinking, *Oh, my God, can I do this? Will she guess how little I know? What if I'm awful at it? What if I'm not a lesbian after all?* What I am *not* thinking about are primary and secondary relationships, sexual theory, and especially not polyamory.

We kiss for a long time on the couch, then go upstairs. By this time it's 2 A.M., and to tell you the truth, we don't do much more before falling asleep. We do, however, have a warm and cuddly conversation the next morning. We describe our fantasy houses. *This*, I remember. (Mine had a wraparound porch and a creek.)

The hard truth of polyamory arises the next day. It turns out that her lover isn't pleased about our encounter. Seems this lover (a prominent lesbian-about-town who greatly intimidates me) had a different vision in mind. By "open relationship," she meant it was OK to have sex with someone passing

the inflatable butch

through town, someone you didn't know and probably would never see again—certainly not someone you liked.

Which brings me to my problem with polyamory. On top of the jealousy, hurt, and damaged egos, how do you work through all the nuanced interpretations, the immeasurable I-thought-you-meants? Frankly, polyamory looks like processing hell.

And what about the little things, the small touches that only lovers know? How do you keep track of who takes milk in her coffee, who drinks it black, who won't touch caffeine? For that matter, stocking your refrigerator must be a nightmare. Sliced turkey for the meat eater, soy milk for the lactose-intolerant, wine for the one not in AA.

And, to be blunt, how do you remember who likes what in bed? This is crucial. "But sweetheart, I thought you *liked* it when I slid my—oops, never mind."

Speaking of bed, what happens if you wake up with an early-to-rise lover but go to bed with a late-to-bed lover? I'm sure sleep deprivation is really going to help you remember who likes what when.

Not that I have to worry about any of this. I mean, even if I could perfect the art of negotiation and memorize countless intimate details, I'd still run up against the same basic problem: finding lovers to be polyamorous with.

I mean, it's impossible enough to find *one* compatible woman, let alone two or three. Someone who can put up with my weird schedule, variable cash

flow, and easily distracted mind. Someone who's stable yet flexible, discerning yet kind, knows her own mind but isn't a control freak. Someone who is spiritual, intellectual, playful, outdoorsy, shares my sense of humor—

Wait! I'm seeing the light here. With polyamory, nobody has to do it all! Lover #1 can be a stable and kind espresso drinker, while lover #2 can be an intellectual, outdoorsy vegetarian. And even if lover #3 is a meat-eating control freak, well, if she's driving me nuts some weekend, I can always flee her place and invite #1 or #2 over to mine.

As long as they aren't with each other.

And my refrigerator is properly stocked.

First-Class Lesbian

Last month I needed to fly home unexpectedly for my great-aunt's funeral. Of course, without an advance purchase discount, I had to pay full fare. There was a silver lining, though: For the return flight, I received a first-class seat at no extra cost.

So after a reflective yet uplifting weekend, I found myself at Newark International Airport, a first-class plane ticket in hand. Entering the building, I waded through a sea of people.

At this point in my life, I should know it's futile trying to calculate which line will move fastest. No matter which one I pick, the people in front of me either have: (a) a six-leg trip involving three continents and five airports; (b) two pieces of oversize luggage that spur a 20-minute argument; or (c) firearms.

Still, as I stood there trying to pick one, I saw a sign that read FIRST-CLASS CHECK-IN. Truth was, I didn't

the inflatable
butch

feel very first-class. Instead of a sleek attaché case, I had a beat-up suitcase, an overstuffed flight bag, an inherited wool coat, plus a small canvas bag containing—yes, this is true—a snack my mom had made for me.

Feeling like an impostor, I walked to the counter and stood there approximately 15 seconds while the attendant finished with the person ahead of me. I handed her my ticket.

"I apologize for the wait," she said, taking my ticket. "Nonstop to Denver. Your luggage is tagged for priority handling. That should speed up its delivery when you arrive."

I didn't know which startled me more—an airline treating my bags with care or the apology for my quarter-of-a-minute wait. Speechless, I nodded my thanks as she gave directions to my gate, where first-class passengers were invited to board at their leisure. A flight attendant ushered me into the front cabin and offered to hang up my coat.

I don't have to jam it into an overhead compartment, I thought, again dazzled by the royal treatment. She showed me to a wide leather seat and asked, "Would you like a drink before takeoff?"

She had to be kidding. Drinks are supposed to arrive an hour into the flight, when you're bouncing through "rough air." But I didn't inform her of this. Instead I asked for a ginger ale.

As I sipped my drink and practiced looking at ease, a woman sat next to me. Now, I have to admit,

the inflatable butch

I'd been hoping to sit next to a Hollywood star like Whoopi Goldberg or Lily Tomlin. I figured I'd strike up a casual yet sincere conversation, discuss mutual interests (I'd make up some if we didn't have any), and by the time we were over Nebraska she'd be inviting me to Palm Springs to watch the golf tournament. But my rowmate wasn't famous, as far as I could tell. Still, it beat being stuck next to a overachiever salesman who'd spend three hours espousing the wonders of ChemBoost vitamins or Veraflex padding.

As we taxied, Chelsea, a flight attendant with a British accent, addressed us over the intercom. I imagined that as her words were piped back to the coach, her voice transformed into rough Brooklyn slang and her name changed to Bertha.

Takeoff was smooth (it was probably bumpy for the folks in coach), and I relaxed. I was offered another drink, asked if I wanted a pillow, and issued complimentary headphones for the movie.

Now, normally I hate flying. I'm usually preoccupied with crashing; I dwell on wind shear, metal fatigue, ice on the wings. But flying first-class, sunk into that cushy seat, a steady stream of beverages at my disposal and pleasant music filling my ears, I thought, *This plane can't crash. It's mechanically perfect, the pilot's skill and intelligence is limitless, and besides, God loves this plane. This plane is a bird. It could fly without an engine, without fuel, without...*

the inflatable butch

My little reverie was interrupted by the flight attendant. "Ms. Orleans?" she said.

"Yes," I said, sitting up. How did she know my name? Was there a family emergency?

"Ms. Orleans, I'd like to tell you about our dinner selections this evening. We have breast of chicken on a bed of wild mushrooms, with new potatoes lightly sautéed in a lemon dill butter. For our second entrée, we are offering filet mignon with a..."

Awestruck, I didn't tune back in until I heard the words "Black Forest cake and complimentary cocktail." I ordered the chicken and a glass of white wine. While the food wasn't as terrific as the elaborate description suggested, it *was* served on real china.

The rest of the flight passed pleasantly. We were on the ground before I knew it, my bags faithfully awaiting me at baggage pickup. But the magic soon faded. I couldn't find my long-term parking ticket, there were construction delays on the highway, and once home, I was greeted by the smell of pungent compost filling my apartment. I sat down at my kitchen table. So much for first-class pampering: Reality was back full force.

But wait, not quite. I still had the snack my mom had packed for me. I pulled out a real New York bagel, homemade brownies, and an apple. Inside she'd even included a note, telling me she loved me.

Now, *that's* first-class.

How to Write a Lesbian Novel

Start with a lesbian. Make her butch, but not too butch. Call her Tyler, Max, Jess, or some other gender-ambiguous name. Give her a well-paying, impressive yet flexible job. Possible choices: architect, landscaper, travel writer, Web site designer. If nothing comes to mind, make her a consultant.

Give her a home. But don't make it much of a home. In fact, probably for tragic reasons, make sure she has never moved in emotionally. A kind of lesbo-bachelor pad, which is OK because she submerges herself in her well-paying, impressive job.

Now it's time for Lesbian #2. She, of course, must be femme, but not too femme. Name her Chris, Kate, Sara, or Joan. No glamorous job for her—instead she's a responsible office manager, textbook editor, or personnel director who has conscientiously built up a nest egg over the last 15 years. Her

house is warm and cozy, but still she is lonely.

Lonely. Yes. They must both be lonely, having suffered a personal tragedy that occurs before the book begins (so that your readers don't have to suffer through it too). It's best if this tragedy is of a romantic quality: Girlfriend has walked out, girlfriend has died, girlfriend has married a guy. Note: If the tragedy is the butch's, it's enough if a dog or truck has died. If the tragedy is the femme's, then her recent discovery of her latent homosexuality (which forces her to break off her seven-year engagement to Mr. Mediocre) works well. Because of this emotional upheaval, neither of them has had sex for several months, even years. This is essential, as will be discussed.

The two of them must somehow meet. This can happen at a party, support group, bar (even though both of them swear they hardly ever go to bars), or local animal shelter (where the butch is working through the loss of her dog).

Having met, they must, of course, bond. As bonding works best over poignant and convoluted events, this is the time to introduce an unsolved murder, abandoned horse, or paranormal event into the storyline. This is also a good place to throw in symbolism.

Next, having suffered together through adversity (if you choose the unsolved murder route, be sure they spend a night huddled together in a cold, damp cellar, eluding the murderer), your heroines must of

the inflatable butch

course have fiery yet heartfelt sex, before which, however, they must confess their nervousness, seeing as so much time has passed since their last physical encounter (see above).

However, as your book must run a minimum of 225 pages, the emotional fallout from the murder, wounded horse, or paranormality must test their incipient love, while at the same time shaking the very foundation of their core beliefs. Therefore, one of them runs off.

At this point, as they question everything they've ever held dear, you introduce the "treasured friend." The treasured friend can be a childhood gal pal (now living in Texas), an empathetic gay male, a wise grandmother from the hills of Kentucky, or if necessary, a trusted ex-lover—as long the breakup was years ago and they can both now laugh about it.

The first two (gal pal and major fag), get paired up with the wounded butch. They must be wildly entertaining, big-hearted characters who loosen up her chrome-plated heart. The grandma and ex-lover say little but speak volumes, often co-opting a cultural heritage not their own in order to do so. They teach the femme to trust her heart, gut, and other anatomical parts.

After their catharses, the characters desperately try to reconnect. As inaccessibility makes passion soar, one character should by now be either trekking in the Andes, excavating ruins in Morocco, or meditating in Bali (funded by the aforementioned nest egg or impressive paycheck). Barring such exotic locales, be sure she has at least moved across town without notifying the post office.

Through a series of lost E-mails, returned letters, and malfunctioning fax machines, the tension mounts, until by divine intervention, sheer coincidence, or the thoughtfulness of an alert lesbian postal employee, the two are reunited.

At this point, the femme gladly gives up her uninspiring job and moves to the butch's cosmopolitan city, where they buy a newly restored Victorian, express their undying devotion for each other, and get a puppy. But first they make mad, passionate love.

Of course.

Garden-Variety Dykes

It's spring again, and in the great tradition of lesbian gardeners everywhere, last month my girlfriend Laurie and I went three-wheeling. That's right: We were in search of a wheelbarrow.

So off we went to MegaMulch Gardening Center, a superstore sporting numerous wheelbarrow makes and models. All came unassembled—their various wheels, frames, and tub sections lying about in a disorderly fashion.

This seemingly straightforward purchase was no simple matter. I, a "P" on the Myers-Briggs personality indicator, do not finalize a decision easily. And Laurie, a Libra, continually balances one set of alternatives against another.

Eventually, however, we chose a model, gathered up its sections, and were on our way—our heads filled with fantasies of contentedly hauling sheep

the inflatable butch

manure, fallen branches, and miscellaneous yard debris.

When we got home and tried to assemble the thing, however, our fantasies took a nosedive. While the "wheel part" fit the "frame part," the "frame part" didn't fit the "tub part." So the next day, it was back to the store. Since we only needed to switch tubs, we left the frame and wheels in the car.

At the customer service desk, Laurie politely explained that the tub part didn't fit the frame part and could we exchange it for the right tub?

The clerk, a harried young woman, didn't follow. "Yes, we can get you a different wheelbarrow," she said, "but we'll need the other pieces."

So I tried to explain. "It comes unassembled. We don't need a whole new wheelbarrow. Just a new tub."

"So you want to *buy* a new tub for your old wheelbarrow?"

Laurie jumped back in. "No, we bought it here yesterday. If we could just talk with someone in the wheelbarrow section—they understand how these parts are sold."

Again, I chimed in. "You see, there are four different models with three sections and…"

At this point, the clerk was convinced it was time to call the gardening section. Over the P.A. system she announced, "Wheelbarrows, call customer service. Wheelbarrows, customer service, please."

A gardening clerk called back on the intercom, loud enough for everyone in line to hear. "What's up?"

the inflatable butch

The service clerk looked at Laurie, looked at me, turned back to the intercom, and started to explain. "There's a couple..." she began.

Then she hesitated. Two women together, as Laurie and I were—that couldn't be a couple. She tried again. "There's a couple of..."

Again she paused. A couple of what?

Finally she blurted, "There's a couple of...*people*...who need to talk with you."

Those tragic hets, I thought. *They tire themselves out so.*

Still, we got our new tub and happily wheeled it out to the car. As I passed the service desk on my way out, I waved to the clerk, hoping that next time she'd keep it simple, merely yelling into the public address system, "Yo! Wheelbarrows? Call customer service. We've got a couple of dykes with a question."

Now, that would be progress.

On the Rocks

A few months back, I got a phone call from Sam, the editor of the gay magazine for which I write. I figured he had a question about my column. Had it been garbled over the modem again? No. Instead he asked, "Do you want two tickets to the Indigo Girls?"

"The Indigo Girls? At Red Rocks?" I gulped. Red Rocks is a beautiful outdoor amphitheater here in Colorado. And the Indigo Girls—well, you know who they are. So who wouldn't want free tickets? Except that after my last show at Red Rocks—which was also the Indigo Girls—I'd sworn I'd never go back there again. Hmm....

As I mulled over the offer, a voice in my head hissed, *You idiot! Don't pass this up! Hell, if you don't want them, I'll take them.*

Momentarily puzzled by the implications of this

the inflatable butch

paradox, I nonetheless went ahead and accepted the tickets.

I immediately called my lover Laurie at work. "Sam just offered us two Indigo Girls tickets for Friday. Wanna go?"

Laurie was properly excited. "Of course!" To lessen transportation hassles, she suggested I call Lori and Martha and see if we could ride with them.

Now, I should mention that Lori is my ex-lover and Martha is her partner. For the sake of clarity, I'll refer to them as Lori 1 and Laurie 2—a literary device of particular help to those of you reading this column out loud. (Martha, however, will not be assigned a number since she is the only Martha in this story.)

Anyway, Laurie 2's suggestion that we ride with Lori 1 and Martha was an excellent one, as Martha is a "Directions Titan"—so adept with north, south, back roads, and exit ramps that I secretly suspect she has a compass surgically implanted in her head. Plus, Lori 1 loves to drive and Laurie 2 loves to be a passenger, so all around it was a great set up.

Except for one thing. Laurie 2 *didn't* know about my last Indigo Girls concert, which I'd gone to with Lori 1 and her grad school friends. That evening? A disaster. Not only were there the standard outdoor concert hassles—despotic security guards, teeming masses, and seats so far back we needed a Hubble telescope to see the band, but we were also surrounded by drunk guys. Of course, these problems

the inflatable butch

were intensified by the fact that Lori 1 and I were on the verge of breaking up. While she was chatting it up with her pals, I felt like an outsider with my own girlfriend.

So, three years after that miserable night, when Laurie 2 suggested that we ride with my old lover, I did hesitate momentarily. But stoically I forged ahead and hoped for the best. The next day, Sam called again. He had two *backstage passes* to meet Emily and Amy. Suddenly, I was very enthusiastic.

The drive to Red Rocks went smoothly, with Martha navigating us to a lesser-used entrance, thus bypassing about 30,000 cars. The walk to the amphitheater was the customary cardiac workout; the line for the women's bathroom long and serpentine. As I was jostled by the crowd, I repeated my mantra, *There is enough room for everyone. There is enough room for everyone...* Waiting near the line-less men's room, I discovered *one* advantage to being straight: You can have your boyfriend scope out the men's room, then duck inside to pee.

After the rest rooms, Lori 1 and Martha went to their seats and Laurie 2 and I to ours, the location of which was a pleasant surprise. We didn't need a Hubble telescope to see the stage (although a pair of binoculars would have been nice), but best of all the people around us weren't loud drunks. In fact, the beverage of choice in our section wasn't Coors but instead iced cappuccino. Times change.

We apparently landed in the celebrity queers

the inflatable
butch

section, with two local activists behind us and another journalist to our right. The music was fine, the view was gorgeous, and as I cuddled up (vertically) with Laurie 2, memories of the last show were washed away, and I even felt a moment or two of serenity and grace.

All too soon the performance was over and it was *time.* Time to meet the Indigo Girls.

Directions for meeting the Indigo Girls after the concert...

That's what the slip of paper in my hand said. I had read it on the way to Red Rocks, but now, as the concert wrapped up, I wondered if it would work. Would we find the right people? Would they have me on their list? Would Laurie 2 and I really make it backstage?

Go to Stage Door Left. It looks like a barn door and is near a T-shirt booth.

Stage Door Left? "Left" as one faces the stage or "left" from the perspective of standing on the stage looking out at the crowd?

Your contact is Geina Horton from Epic Records. (She has long red hair, allegedly.) If you have questions, ask for any security person.

As the final cheers faded and the floodlights were thrown on, Laurie 2 and I began our trek toward the stage. Spotting a T-shirt booth—there was one on *each* side of the stage—I collared the first security guard I saw. He had no idea who Geina was and showed no interest in assisting me. In a momentary

panic I wondered if it was Geina herself—and not just her long red hair—that was "alleged." But then a butchy female guard leaned over the railing and advised, "Try finding someone with a walkie-talkie."

I did that, locating an intelligent-looking security person who whipped out her walkie-talkie and quickly made contact. I sighed, smitten with her competency. She led us to the barnlike door.

There Geina (and her alleged hair) greeted us and thanked me (yes, *she* thanked *me*) for coming. She gave us each a cool-looking backstage pass with a snake on it. We were then told to wait across the way, along with two dozen others. Clearly, this was not going to be a private meeting.

I admit, the previous day I had practiced insightful yet casual observations to share with the Indigo Girls—metaphor in their lyrics, their impact on contemporary rock—things like that. I even planned places to go just in case they wanted to go out for a late dinner.

Now, as the group of backstage-pass holders grew, I adjusted my fantasy: I practiced being insightful and *brief*.

As we waited, a woman who looked like an extra from *Go Fish* walked past, took one look, and disdainfully commented, "Groupies."

"Jealous," Laurie 2 and I both agreed. Besides, we were far from being groupies. Neither of us had brought along a camera, nor did we have CDs or publicity photos for the Girls to sign. I had, however,

the inflatable
butch

brought two copies of my book to give them.

At last, Geina called us forward in small groups. When Laurie 2 and I reached the door, the guard said, "Orleans plus one."

"I'm Orleans," I said.

"I'm 'plus one,'" Laurie 2 added.

And we were inside. Step one completed. My group was led downstairs to a large room. Geina instructed the crowd, "There are a lot of you, and Amy and Emily only have a half hour, so please only one photograph and one autograph from each of them. They should be here soon."

Geina continued making notes on her clipboard. "Pretty mellow show, huh?" I commented.

"Yeah, I've been doing Metallica shows all week," she said. "This is a nice break."

As I set my books on the table, I noticed that once again a group of cute dykes was seated next to Laurie 2. (For some inexplicable reason, good-looking women gravitate toward her.) One of the women asked to see a copy of my book. The group laughed as they read it, and I basked in my 15 nanoseconds of fame.

Then Amy and Emily strolled in, said a casual "Hi, y'all," and greeted people they knew. I thought they looked older than their pictures, and Laurie 2 thought they looked shorter.

When it was our turn to say hello, Amy and Emily were genuine, gracious, and sweet—none of that "I'm so bored" attitude. They thanked me for

my book, and Amy even said she'd seen it in an Atlanta bookstore.

Suddenly, it was over and time to go. So although meeting the Indigo Girls had not lived up to my wild fantasies, I decided it had been fun—definitely something to write home about.

Then, just as Laurie 2 and I were about to leave the room, Amy called out, "Laurie, Ellen! Stick around for a few minutes, and we can go out for a late dinner. It would be great to get to know you better. Plus, I'd love to discuss lyrics with you."

Emily added, "And if you have any friends, be sure to ask them along."

Ahem. Only in my dreams. Only in my dreams.

The Inflatable Butch

While traveling by plane, I love to flip through the complimentary catalog of upscale products. This month, I was quite taken with "Safe-T Man: Your Superior Bodyguard."

According to the catalog, Safe-T Man is "a life-size, simulated male that appears to be 180 lbs. and 6 feet tall." Made of inflatable vinyl, he "gives others the impression that you have the protection of a male guardian in your home or car." All this for only $99.95, repair patch included. (The dual-action pump is sold separately.)

Safe-T Man looks incredibly real—or so claims the copy—with his posable latex hands and airbrushed facial highlights. But my favorite line in Safe-T Man's description is "When not keeping vigil, Safe-T Man can be deflated, stored, and transported in an optional tote bag." Ah, were all men so easy.

the inflatable butch

Even though he's marketed as a bodyguard, this fellow has a multitude of practical applications. Closeted lesbian couples could use Safe-T Man as Cover-Man. That's right, just stick him on a recliner in front of ESPN; then, if friends from work unexpectedly drop by, you can point out to your guests that your "man" is in the TV room, engrossed in the game, while you and your "friend" practice various massage strokes on each other.

Bopping around town with Safe-T Man in your car, you'd not only add to your heterosexual front, but you'd also be complimented for choosing a sensitive New Age guy who's safe enough in his masculinity to let you drive.

Of course, what I'm waiting for is not Safe-T man, but Safe-T Butch, the inflatable diesel dyke bodyguard. Dress her in black jeans and work boots, stick a wrench in one of those posable latex hands, and nobody's gonna mess with either of you.

But that's just the beginning. Need a quick date for a party? Just pull Safe-T Butch out of her tote bag and inflate away. Some friends may wonder why your new gal doesn't say much, but most folks know that old-school butches just aren't big talkers.

Is your old girlfriend snooping around your house, peeking in windows to see if you've got a new honey pot? Viewed through the window shade, Safe-T Butch will throw your ex off-kilter, convincing her you've moved on to greener, albeit quieter, pastures.

But full-size plastic folks aren't the only ones for

the inflatable butch

sale. Surely you know of Billy, the first gay doll. GI Joe on steroids, this doll comes with cowboy, leatherman, sailor, and vacation outfits. And the catalog promises that Billy is anatomically complete.

Just how complete? I wasn't sure until I happened upon a Billy doll in Key West's Flaming Maggie's. There I found a brunette version of Billy (he's also available in platinum blond) clothed only in a pair of tiny black leather chaps, his anatomically complete member boldly on display. So how big is Billy? Simply put, he's hung like a horse. Proportionally, that is. Realistically, I had to feel sorry for the guy. Imagine if he were advertising in the personals: "Thick-chested gay white doll seeks companion for mutual admiration, exchange of outfits, and more. Me: Good-looking, clean-shaven, 1-inch dick."

Which of course makes me wonder about Safe-T Man. How anatomically complete is this "incredibly realistic" fellow? And if he is, does that part of him require the dual-action pump?

All of which may make you wonder why I, a certified lesbian, am writing in such detail about a gay doll. Because, of course, I'm dreaming up the first out lesbian doll: Liz. Strong, competent, and visually striking, Liz is as comfortable in lipstick and power pumps as she is in flannel and running shoes. An accountant who can fix leaky faucets *and* cook a killer lasagna, Liz does it all. With eager women lined up around the block, Liz doesn't need a personal ad, but if she did run one, it would sound something like

this: "Self-assured lesbian doll seeks soul mate for marathon training, foreign films, gourmet cooking. Me: smooth skin, firm breasts, $\frac{1}{16}$-inch clit."

The Hard, Cold Truth

The path of a writer is a rocky, if not tortured journey: soul-searching nights, endless rejection letters, pitiful financial rewards. Yet, every now and then, a distinct if faint light appears, buoying up our creative spirits, our artistic resolve.

Such a light shone for me the other day in the form of a prominent award. No, I wasn't notified of any Lambda Literary Award nominations or told I'd received the Pulitzer.

No, it was much greater than that.

You see, I won Honorable Mention in the—*drum roll, please*—Ben & Jerry's "Yo! I'm Your CEO" contest!

Ben & Jerry's CEO contest? What the hell is she talking about?

Allow me to explain. As you probably know, Ben & Jerry's has grown from a pop-and-pop shop in

Burlington, Vermont, to an international multimillion-dollar concern. A few years back, the founders—playful guys with groovy politics—realized they needed to hire a savvy corporate-minded CEO to free themselves to concentrate on the fun stuff, like promoting their traveling circus, picking acts for their folk festival and, of course, coming up with new names for their ever-expanding line of ice cream and frozen yogurt.

Always imaginative, they decided to have some fun with the job hunt. In addition to the serious search, they held a nationwide contest. Anyone who wanted to be considered for the position only had to write, in 100 words or less, why they should be Ben & Jerry's next CEO. That was it! (Oh, yeah, you also had to send in a lid from your favorite flavor.)

So, last summer, while at the Jersey shore with my family, I picked up information about the contest, and one night while everyone sat around schmoozing, I perched in the corner, obsessively tapping away on my PowerBook.

When I returned to Boulder, I heard that the company had already received thousands of entries. Intimidated yet undaunted, I toiled on, revising my piece until I came up with my final submission:

"Ben & Jerry's Needs a Chief"
(Sung to the tune of "Old MacDonald Had a Farm")
Ben and Jerry's needs a chief.
C-E, C-E-O !

the inflatable butch

Qualifications? I'll keep mine brief.
C-E, C-E-O !

With design and graphics here,
And teaching students there,
Here some writing,
There some speaking,
Every job a "creative undertaking!"
C-E, C-E-O !

So please don't hire a stuffed-shirt hack.
C-E, C-E-O !
Just because she or he can keep you in the black!
C-E, C-E-O !

With a global vision here,
And a personal sacrifice there:
Sampling for lunch
A dish of Pinecone Crunch,
Every day, a new idea to munch!
Yo! I'm your C-E-O!

Finally and gallantly, I consumed a pint of Chunky Monkey, rinsed its lid, and popped it—along with my poem—into a large envelope, which I deposited at the post office.

Then I forgot about it.

But then, two days ago a box with the words "Ben & Jerry's Peace Pops" appeared in my mail. Rummaging through, I discovered that I, along with

only 99 other brilliant people, had been awarded an Honorable Mention in the contest!! Yes, out of more than 25,000 entries, I received an official rejection letter. In part, it read:

Congratulations! You did a great job on your application for CEO. It warms our hearts—and blows our minds—that someone of your high caliber would even consider a career with us. That said, it is with mixed ingredients that we give you the bad news and the good news. The bad news is you didn't get the CEO job. The good news, however, is you didn't get the CEO job. Whew!

But now you can tell your children and grandchildren you came this close to running our company. To say you're overqualified might seem like a cheap kiss-off. So let's just say that your talents and potential convinced us that a much higher calling awaits you. Yo! Go, and follow your destiny! You're just too valuable to the world to be peddling ice cream.

Besides this heartwarming full-color official rejection letter, what else did I win? First, a groovy shirt that says, SOMEONE ELSE GOT CEO, BUT I GOT THIS SWELL T-SHIRT! Also, a Ben & Jerry's pencil, a White Russian refrigerator magnet, and a bumper sticker that reads, IF IT'S NOT FUN, WHY DO IT?

There was also a postcard of the original Ben & Jerry's store—a converted gas station. I remember

the inflatable butch

going there in the late '70s with my brother Bill. The place was just starting out and featured a full menu: burgers, fries, pizza, and desserts. My brother said, "Try their ice cream. It's really good."

And finally, I received a coupon for a free pint of ice cream, which I plan to put to use very soon. What flavor, you ask? Their latest coffee concoction: Coffee Heath Bar Crunch. I figure that between the caffeine and the sugar I should be up all night, following my destiny as I seek that higher calling that undoubtedly awaits me.

To the Rescue

Dear Friend,
Thank you for your interest in National Lesbian Rescue, America's leading organization for the rescue and rehabilitation of dykes. Similar to Greyhound Rescue, Farm Horse Rescue, and Groundhog Rescue, our mission is to remove lesbians from undesirable situations and place them in positive atmospheres to stimulate and nurture their personal and political growth. We hope the following information will help you decide whether taking a lesbian into your home or office is the right choice for you.

Where does National Lesbian Rescue find its lesbians?
Sadly, neglected lesbians can be found all throughout the United States. Following up on anonymous phone calls and unconfirmed gossip, our

the inflatable butch

impassioned volunteers scour corporate high-rises, military bases, and local convents for needy lesbians. Our award-winning neighborhood watch group searches block by block for potential lesbians stuck in loveless hetero marriages.

What does Lesbian Rescue do with lesbians once they find them?

Once lesbians are located, they spend a month at our luxurious Rescue Ranch, where they can run free in their natural state. Furthermore, our lesbians are pampered with massages, hot tubs, gourmet meals, and a full library of queer books and videos. From there, they are matched up with work and living situations to best suit their individual needs.

Who are some of the lesbians Lesbian Rescue has helped?

One of our earliest success stories is Catherine Joan McIver, discovered just north of Omaha. Previously a low-ranking saleswomon for a multilevel marketing company, after just two weeks at the Rescue Ranch, Catherine Joan changed her name to C.J., had a fling with the local groundskeeper, and became a videographer. Her work is now represented by a trendy retro gallery in the East Village.

Does Lesbian Rescue only rescue newly out or deeply closeted lesbians?

Not at all. Recently, Lesbian Rescue liberated

the inflatable
butch

Marjorie Hammaker, a tenured queer studies professor in San Francisco. Although she appeared to have everything—a cutting-edge career, the respect of her colleagues, and a $700,000 home in Sausalito—what Marjorie really wanted to do was bake bread. Last month, with the help of Lesbian Rescue, she was placed in a small dyke-owned bakery in Missoula, Montana. She reports she couldn't be happier.

Does Lesbian Rescue only work with left-wing, anti-establishment lesbians?

While Lesbian Rescue was started by radical fire-breathing Sapphists and remains committed to the total domination of the planet by dykes, we also believe in individual choice for all wimmin. That's why Lesbian Rescue was there within hours when Fireweed Bravewomon called for help. Since 1972, Fireweed had been living in a lesbian-only, consensus-governed, macrobiotic log cabin near Ann Arbor, Michigan. She needed out. Badly. Within 24 hours, Fireweed was relocated to Rescue Ranch, where she promptly changed her name to Florence, learned line dancing, and became a spokeswomon for the National Beef Council.

Can my donation be earmarked for a specific lesbian?

Because the cost of feeding, bathing, and providing feminine-hygiene products for the residents of Rescue Ranch is so high, Lesbian Rescue always

the inflatable butch

appreciates undesignated donations. But we also know many contributors prefer directed giving. For this reason, in 1998 we established the nation's first "Save a Lesbian" program. Each "Save a Lesbian" sponsor is assigned a specific lesbian who needs a new home, job, or lover. Her sponsor is then free to give help in whatever way she can.

Are there lesbians who are especially in need?

Yes. This year we are working with a special group in dire circumstances: Hollywood lesbians. Once megastars and huge box-office draws, these lesbians have been abandoned by inhumane agents and callous casting directors. Unfulfilled and unemployable, they desperately need glamorous homes in the Aspen/Vail area in which to live out their final decades or at least bide their time until TV lesbians become fashionable again.

I'm convinced! How can I help?

In addition to monetary contributions, job opportunities, and free housing, Rescue Ranch needs wimmin to feed, bathe, and possibly have sex with our rescued lesbians. Please check off the appropriate boxes on the enclosed donor card.

Yours in sisterhood,
   The Wimmin of National Lesbian Rescue,
   where our slogan is "Rescued today, radical
   tomorrow!

As the Wheels Spin (Part I)

For Sale: '79 Honda Civic Hatchback. 144,000 miles, runs strong. Dark blue exterior with dented hood. Light blue interior with minor raccoon damage. Classic-style steering wheel, AM/FM cassette, glove box that opens every sixth try. Great bumper stickers. $450 or best offer.

When my Honda passed its emissions test the other day, I told it, "Good job! Now I can sell you."

Immediately, I was ashamed by my words. It was as if I had told my child, "Good job! You've cleaned your room, washed the dishes, and taken out the trash. Now I'm going to pawn you off on some other family."

Clearly, I'm attached to my car. When I bought it

the inflatable butch

in 1985, I'd just turned 24. I was living with three roommates, earning $4.15 an hour at an art supply store, and wasn't yet out, not even to myself. Eleven years later, I've lived in eight homes, held six jobs, had two long-term relationships and an undisclosed number of short-term ones. Throughout it all, only my car has remained constant.

I remember the day I bought it. My friend Annie drove me to the home of its owner, where we signed papers, exchanged money, and shook hands. As I was getting ready to go, he placed a finger beside his nostril and made a sniffing noise. Thinking he was clearing his sinuses, I continued toward the door. Annie, ever more sophisticated than I, stopped me. "He's asking if you want to do a line of coke. To celebrate."

Coke? I thought. *Are you crazy? I'm about to drive away in my first car, an unfamiliar car—an unfamiliar standard-transmission car—and, oh, by the way, I have a grand total of two hours experience using a clutch. You expect me to do that on a cocaine buzz?!*

I politely declined.

At work, discussion was dominated by what to name my new purchase. The concept of auto appellations was new to me, having grown up in a household bereft of such practices. Our cars were simply referred to as "Dad's car," "Mom's car," or "the station wagon." Functional, but uninspired.

After a few days with no brilliant ideas, I felt

frustrated. Annie assured me that car names can't be thought up; they simply must "arrive." That afternoon, as I was ordering art books for the store, inspiration hit. I named my car "Bowker," after R.R. Bowker, one the publishers from whom I ordered. Bowker had a nice toddler sound to it, and my Honda reminded me of a little kid.

Of course, the name Bowker didn't solve the gender dilemma. Was my car a he or a she? My co-workers wanted to know. (Underemployment causes smart people to become engrossed in amazingly inane matters.)

After two months of continual mechanical problems, I decided it was a "he," since only males could be that much trouble. As time went on, though, Bowker ceased to fit neatly into either a male or female category. I guess it's a transgender/ transmission kind of thing.

Once I began taking my car to a real mechanic—as opposed to whatever place was sending out coupons that week—the Honda became dependable. Still, it has had its moments. One summer, my friend Katya (who was pregnant at the time) and I went camping, driving up roads intended solely for off-road vehicles.

Because its motor was so hot, Bowker was experiencing vapor lock and having a hard time starting. (Actually, I have no idea why it had a hard time starting. Vapor lock just sounds impressively technical.) Anyway, as I was driving up a Jeep road in first gear,

the inflatable butch

a chipmunk trotted in front of the car. I knew that if I braked, the car would stall, and I'd have to start it at a treacherous 30-degree incline. But if I didn't break, I'd hit the chipmunk, who was staring, immobile, at me. I honked, I yelled, and I finally braked, immediately after which the chipmunk took off.

Of course, the car wouldn't start. Instead it slid backward. After two or three tries, I told Katya to get out of the car. "If I end up going off the side of the mountain," I declared solemnly, "I don't want to take you and the baby with me." She got out, and I banked the car against the mountainside and got it going again.

Seven months later, Katya's son Zeke was born. Bowker and I had the honor of driving him and his parents home. With the infant seat strapped in, I drove out of the hospital parking lot. As we moved onto the street, Katya leaned over and whispered, "Ellen, it's OK to go more than six miles an hour."

"Are you kidding?" I told her. "I'm driving a newborn baby. My tank of gas is older than this kid! I have to be very, very careful." Eventually, I revved up to 15 mph, safely depositing the three of them at their home.

As the years passed, I've used the name Bowker less and less, instead simply calling my Honda "the car." Mostly, I talk to it with endearments such as "baby" and "sweetheart." You see, my Honda and I have merged. We've grown up together. The driver's seat has molded to the contours of my back, the

the inflatable butch

clutch shifts into third only for me, and the bumper stickers reflect my evolving politics.

My very first adornment in this area was a non-controversial choice: a window decal from my college. Being a *Star Trek* fan, I soon adhered a Starfleet Academy decal next to it. I regret that I have no record of my very first bumper sticker, but I remember my first gay one: I'M ONE TOO. Once a pile of women in a compact Toyota pulled alongside me on the highway and yelled, "So are we!"

My Honda has survived several physical indignities. One winter, a snowplow slid on a patch of ice and smashed up the back. I toyed with the idea of using the $800 insurance settlement for something fun, like a trip to a very warm place, but ended up repairing the damage. I think the car appreciated it.

Two years ago my Honda and I were in our first serious accident. I got hit on the interstate, and the car did a 180. But I was OK and so was the car. *We* were OK. A deep bonding experience.

But now it's time to let go. My brother has given me his old car. It has 30,000 fewer miles, fifth gear, air conditioning, and cruise control. I plan to actually drive it—gasp—out of state. Eventually, I trust, we too will bond.

So that's it. Oh, the raccoon damage? That's another story.

As the Wheels Spin (Part II)

Greetings! Welcome to your personal tour of my new car. Come, sit in the passenger seat as I point out the luxury features of my Honda Accord.

In front of you, you'll find the glove compartment. Press the button. It opens! Close it, it stays shut. Miraculous, huh? Another major technical innovation is the rear trunk. See this lever? Lift it and—pop! The trunk opens. Cool, huh? But wait, there's more. Roll up the driver's side window and—it fits snugly! No rattling, no mini snowstorms blowing in.

What? Not impressed? You undoubtedly did not know my previous car with its nonpoppable hatch, unpredictable glove compartment, and loose windows that offered surprise showers at the drive-through car wash.

the inflatable butch

I must confess, however, that my new car is only new to me. To the rest of the world it's just a 1985 Honda. But I don't care. When I drive it, I'm behind the wheel of a Lexus.

As satisfied as I am with my new used car, it was not love at first sight. Letting go of my '79 Honda was traumatic—and confusing. After the sale, as I watched the new owner drive off, two thoughts ran through my head: (1) *What's he doing? That's my car!* and (2) *Good Lord, that automobile looks like it's about to fall apart.* (Apparently, my friends have been thinking the same thing for years.)

With my Civic gone, it was time to make friends with the Accord. During our first two weeks, I had serious reservations. My new car wasn't as peppy as my hatchback, and I couldn't squeeze it into tight parking places or hang a sharp U-turn.

I did, however, overcome one barrier early on: what to name it. My brother earned the money for *his* new vehicle by filming commercials for Calistoga Waters—I know, you're terribly impressed—which allowed him to give me his old car. Hence, in honor of Calistoga, I christened my new car "Cali."

But even Cali's cool name couldn't overcome the fact that I, Ellen Orleans—writer, Bohemian, and dedicated disregarder of conventional standards—was driving a *gray four-dour sedan*! Every time I looked at this car, I half expected to find a family of four in the backseat, golf clubs and groceries in the trunk.

Also, it wasn't until I owned one that I realized

the inflatable butch

that every tenth car in Boulder is a gray four-door. Not only did I begin losing my car in parking lots at an incredible rate, but at work I even tried opening someone else's trunk.

Another time, emerging from my mechanic with a bill for $650, I firmly addressed Cali, "OK, you now have fresh oil, new front brakes, two new spark plugs, rotated tires, and replaced hoses. I expect you to stay in good shape for the next 12 months." It wasn't until I went to unlock the door that I realized I was talking to somebody else's car. I heard Cali snicker behind my back.

During the first month, I desperately missed the individuality of my old car. But you know what they say: "Be careful what you ask for—you may get it." You see, as part of her overall design, Cali has more legroom than my Civic. That's great for people who are 5 foot 5 and over, but as I am part of the 5-foot-and-under set, more legroom only means more distance to the pedals. Driving, especially clutching, was uncomfortable.

Since growing three additional inches was out of the question (I've tried; it doesn't work), I looked into having the driver's seat floor tracks moved forward. Too expensive. Standard racing car extenders? Too long. Finally, my mechanic came up with a brilliant idea. Hockey pucks! Yes, he bolted one hockey puck each to the gas, brake, and clutch, thus solving two problems at once. My car was easier to drive, and now it was unique.

Well, on the inside anyway. On the outside, Cali definitely needed distinguishing markings. Yes, bumper stickers. Plowing through a mail-order catalog, I came across a set of rather amusing ones. It began with the standard: AGAINST ABORTION? DON'T HAVE ONE, then offered the gentler AGAINST ABORTION? SUPPORT FAMILY PLANNING. It in turn was followed by the in-your-face AGAINST ABORTION? HAVE A VASECTOMY.

To which I'd like to add my own version: AGAINST ABORTION? PROMOTE HOMOSEXUALITY.

If nothing else, having that on my bumper would cut my parking-space search time way, way down.

Whose Cat?

So you and your lover have decided to move in together. Got yourselves a cozy place with just enough space for each of you to hold onto your individual identities. That's great. And you'll both be sharing each other's stuff, of course. Her mattress and CD player, your cordless phone and Krups espresso maker. Yup, you've got everything worked out just fine.

But wait, aren't you forgetting something? Need a hint? It's small, soft...has a tail. That's right, you're also moving in with your lover's cat. And that brings up the question, just whose cat is this? Is it hers or now both of yours?

My lover and I had the same questions when we decided to cohabitate. But, fortunately, within a few months I was able to easily determine the answer to the "our cat/her cat" question. And having made this

the inflatable
butch

vital discovery, I'd like to pass the information on to you. (For the purposes of this demonstration, we will use the generic cat name "Whiskers.") Ready?

When Whiskers strikes a cute position with one paw raised and her tongue part way out, she's "our cat." When Whiskers trots outside, eats grass, trots back in, and throws up, she's "her cat." Cuddles up close in the middle of a winter's night?—"our cat." Walks on your head at 3 A.M.?—"her cat."

Getting the hang of it now? Let's try a few more. Dutifully uses her scratching post—"our cat." Shreds the curtains—"her cat." Sits lightly on your stomach, purring contentedly—"our cat." Sits with her butt in your face—"her cat."

Is she playfully chasing her catnip toy, delicately lapping milk from her bowl, lying on her back while you rub her stomach? Then she's "our cat, our cat, our cat." Time to change the kitty litter? Buy another bag of Iams? Pay for the feline leukemia shots? Now it's "her cat, her cat, her cat."

See, it's pretty easy. If you feel, however, that it's too complicated to keep track of this ever-changing hers-and-ours business, just remember one simple rule: During shedding season, its always *her* cat.

The Out Scout

Were you a Girl Scout? C'mon, raise those hands!

I was. Briefly. However, unlike other dykes' lurid tales of girl-on-girl exploring beneath mildewy cotton sleeping bags, my scouting days were obsessively focused on earning merit badges, those round emblems of a virtuous, if slightly dykey, girlhood. I longed to be like Marybeth Watkins, whose collection of badges began mid-sash, parading boastfully downward before swaggering high up the back. Each badge was meticulously sewn into place, perfectly aligned. Me? I never got past eight badges, which I glued on with Elmer's.

Jumping ahead a few decades, I was thinking, since so many lesbians were nurtured in the cradle of scouting, why not have merit badges for us grown-ups?

the inflatable butch

Coming-Out Badge

Complete at least one of the following:
1. Come out to yourself.
2. Come out to the relative of your choice.
3. Out the relative of your choice.

Rad-Les-Fem Badge

Complete two of the following:
1. Dress as La Femme Nikita for the office barbecue.
2. Cross-dress as your male boss for the office barbecue.
3. Drive ten miles in a hailstorm to a women's bookstore to buy a book that you could have purchased at Barren & Ignoble for $3 less.
4. Special-order lesbian porn from your neighborhood Christian bookstore.

Personal Growth Badge

1. Obtain at least three of the following:
   - a feisty bumper sticker
   - steel-toed boots
   - a lacy bra
   - a prominent tattoo
   - a spiritual practice
   - a vibrator

2. Complete at least one of each in the following pairs:
   - Endure 12 roommates, six cats, three dogs,

and half a refrigerator shelf for eight years.
- Walk out on all of them and buy a condo.
- Sleep with your best friend.
- Swear to never again wreck a good friendship with sex.
- Attend your first lover's commitment ceremony.
- Attend your first lover's commitment ceremony to your previous girlfriend. Bonus points!
- Decide at age 60 to enter therapy.
- Decide at age 40 that 20 years of therapy is enough and fly to Paris for the weekend.

Relationships Badge
1. Fall in love with a woman for the first time.
2. Get dumped.
3. Take her back.
4. Together, experience monogamy, serial non-monogamy, polyamory, group sex, and couples counseling (not necessarily in that order).

Body-Image Badge
Do as many as you want:
1. Celebrate your first skinned knee as a born-again jock.
2. Trim your nails.
3. Grow your nails (and apply silver polish).
4. Don't shave your legs.

5. Do shave your head.
6. Start lifting weights.
7. Stop dieting.
8. Nurture your chin hairs.
9. Go topless:
   (a) in a pride parade.
   (b) in Provincetown.
   (c) in downtown New York—does anyone notice?

But why stop with these themes? Why not reclaim those old merit badges for our own purposes? With a simple word swap here and there, it's easy!

Active-Citizen Badge

1. Show how to use and care for the American rainbow flag. (Does the red stripe go on the top or the bottom? Does anyone care if it touches the ground?)

2. Explain how a person becomes a citizen of the U.S.A. Lesbian Nation and how a person may lose her citizenship.

3. Find out about government dyke agencies that serve you and your family. Visit one of them. Meet the board members. Flirt with the treasurer. Volunteer for the fund-raising committee. Note subconsciously that your girlfriend is miffed. Spend more time volunteering. After the annual fund-raiser, count the cashbox late at night—with the treasurer. Toss the tens, twenties, and personal checks to the floor and

have mad sex on the folding table. Return home to find your relationship bankrupt. Find out about some of the dyke agencies that serve single lesbians.

Hospitality Badge

1. Discuss with your dyke cohorts the different ways to recruit new lesbians and win back reprobates engaging in (gasp!) bisexuality or transgenderism.

2. List three things you should do as an overnight guest. Compare lists, then after a trial run or two, determine which local lesbians offer a well-stocked refrigerator, a decently scrubbed shower, and the latest in sex-toy technology. Hope that none of your lesbian guests is compiling a list about you.

3. Practice making introductions correctly: a new girl to your troop; a straight girl to your queer theater troop; your gay ex-husband to your father's second wife; your 1996 sperm donor to your 2001 sperm donor; your new—and male—lover to your parents; current copresidents of your hometown PFLAG.

4. Put on a skit showing courteous telephone manners for the following occasions:
   (a) Coming out to your grandmother (for the third time).
   (b) Explaining to your girlfriend how you accidentally slept with her sister.
   (c) Informing the hotel clerk that you want one room for two women with one— that's right, just one—queen-size bed.

And don't forget these classic badges!

Cooking Badge
Prepare all of the following at least once:
1. Real food for a potluck. (Chips and salsa don't count.)
2. An aphrodisiac appetizer to be eaten in bed. (No utensils permitted!)
3. Basic omelettes for the morning after.

Sewing Badge
Choose two:
1. Sew a rainbow patch to your daypack.
2. Hem your butch girlfriend's Dockers.
3. Repair the seam of your femme girlfriend's cocktail dress (and prove that a butch gal can use a needle and thread, thank you very much). If this is not possible, instead oil and lube a Singer sewing machine.

And finally...

Lesbian Explorer Badge
Set your own criteria, break a few rules, and be sure to let us know how it turns out.

Taxes and Gefilte Fish: A Passover Story

Last week I was startled to realize that Passover and tax time occur at roughly the same time of year. Now, you might not see the incredible coincidence in this—after all, Passover is a celebration of freedom and rebirth, while tax time is a season of dread and remorse over shoddy bookkeeping habits. Yet, as I began preparing my return, a childhood Passover ritual came to mind, and suddenly the relationship between these two sacred events was crystalized.

It all started with memories of the search for leavened bread or *chamatz*, which is pronounced by making a brief gargling sound, then saying "mates." (Guess you'll just have to wait for the audio edition.) You see, according to tradition, during Passover no foods containing leavened flour are

the inflatable butch

allowed in the home. So what are Jewish families supposed to do with their rye bread, Entemann's pastries, and rigatoni?

Well, back in the old country (or so the story goes), the Jews gathered up such food and gave it away. Of course, in 1970s suburban New Jersey where I grew up, it was a little trickier. I can't quite picture my family driving over to the local mall and passing out half-empty boxes of Ritz crackers and loaves of Wonder Bread. My mom ended up stashing much of it in the freezer.

But back to tradition. The night before Passover begins (all Jewish holidays start in the evening—it's a lunar thing) there's a ceremonial search for any last crusts. It's kind of like an Easter egg hunt, except it will never take place on the White House lawn. When I was growing up, my dad would hide pieces of a bagel, after which we kids hunted them down with a dustpan and broom.

But whether it was my great-great-etc.-grandmother in Russia cleaning between the floorboards or my mother scrubbing with Top Job, the result was the same: Passover cleansing becomes spring cleaning.

So what the heck does this have to do with taxes? Well, last week, while Jewish families around the globe were searching for bread, I was searching for business receipts. While most were in my accordion folder, I was fully aware that a slew of errant receipts lay hidden elsewhere, just waiting to be discovered.

the inflatable butch

And discover them I did, neatly folded in my wallet, stuffed in the recesses of my Day-Timer, serving as bookmarks in unfinished novels. In my search for tax write-offs, I searched through old Visa statements, duplicate check stubs, and lots of drawers (including silverware and sock drawers).

Amid this paper hurricane, I felt a sudden desire to recycle the edifice of newspapers growing under my desk, to arrange and label my computer diskettes, to even, yes, reorganize my filing cabinet! Initially, I considered this simply a technique for avoiding my taxes, but then revelation struck! Just as Passover is the impetus for kitchen cleaning, tax time is the stimulus for office rebirth.

The Passover seder itself is a ritual-packed meal containing as many courses as it does prayers. In fact, *seder* is Hebrew for *order*. So as I began filling out tax forms, I was again stunned by similarities: The word *order* kept leaping into my brain.

Consider this: During the seder, there are very specific times for asking the four questions, reciting the ten plagues, and eating the gefilte fish. It's the same with taxes! I start by filling out the popular 1040, but at line 12 where it asks for business income, I beat a hasty retreat to Schedule C. My efforts pay off until line 13, where I have to fill in depreciation figures, so I head to Form 4562, then back to 1040—well, you get the picture. The whole thing reminds me of "Had Gadya," a song about a goat that we sing at the end of the seder: "Then came

ellen orleans

the stick that beat the dog that bit the cat that ate the goat my father bought for two *zuzim*."

My version? "Then came the Schedule SE that satisfied Line 25 that completed Schedule C that contained line 13 that needed Form 4562 that will bring us back to 'doe!' Doe, a deer, a female..." Oops. Wrong song.

I could go on drawing comparisons, but it wouldn't be fair. Figuring one's taxes isn't really like wandering in the desert for 40 years—it just feels that way. And various IRS evils (self-employment tax, limits on home/office use) don't really measure up to the magnitude of vermin, locusts, or any of the other ten plagues. (Then again, considering what the military does with our money...)

But finally, there comes that moment when the final calculator key is pressed, the final box filled in. Suddenly, the Red Sea parts and a completed tax form emerges! Next Year in Jerusalem!

Next year...it all goes to an accountant.

Sharing the Faith

One morning not long ago, I was hanging out on my bed, grading student papers, wearing nothing more than a T-shirt and underwear, when suddenly there was a knock at my door.

I sat up, craned my neck, and looked out the window to see two well-coiffed, heavily made-up females. Naturally, my first thought was, *What are two drag queens doing at my door at this hour?* Then reality set in: Jehovah's Witnesses! Instantly, I froze. Could they tell I was home or did the glare from the window block their view?

Slowly, I slid under the covers. They knocked again. A patient but firm knock. Inside me, a voice scolded, *You coward! This is your house! Get up and answer the door!* I visualized striding confidently across my living room, swinging open the door, and fearlessly confronting them.

the inflatable butch

"We see you're Jewish," they'd say, pointing to the mezuzah by the door, "but you *can* be saved. Let's talk a moment about redemption through Jehovah's kingdom."

"Let's not," I'd respond. "Five thousand years of proselytizing is plenty, thanks."

Or perhaps they'd ask, "Sister, do you know Jesus Christ?"

"Know him?" I'd reply. "Why we just had lunch yesterday!"

But no. Instead I remained inert until they headed to the upstairs neighbors. Then, crouching down, I escaped into the bathroom, safely hidden in case they knocked again on the return trip.

Later, it occurred to me that as annoying as Jehovah's Witnesses are, I do admire their persistence. It takes a lot of guts to go door to door, day after day, being terminally perky about your faith.

Heck, I thought, if they can do it, why can't we? Why can't we be the "JeHomo's" Witnesses, testifying, converting, and otherwise butting into other people's lives?

Imagine it. Pairs of gay men and lesbians, heading off to the suburbs, right around suppertime. The rest would go something like this:

Christopher and Louise, two seasoned JeHomo's Witnesses, walk up to a split-level home and ring the doorbell. A harried husband answers the door.

the inflatable butch

Louise: Hello, sir. We're JeHomo's Witnesses. May we come in?

Husband: Sorry, we're Unitarians. We're not interested in switching religions.

Christopher: Oh, no, sir. We wouldn't dream of asking you to switch religions. Just your sexual orientation.

Louise: Yes, we're JeHomo's, not Jehovah's, Witnesses. We're here to spread the good news about homosexuality.

Husband: Huh? Maybe you should speak to my wife. Sally!

Wife: I'm in the middle of dinner, Frank—oh, hi. Who are you?

Louise: I'm Louise and this is Christopher.

Husband: They're JeHomo's Witnesses.

Wife: [*catty*] Nice of you to stop by, but I can take care of my own afterlife, thank you.

Louise: Oh, it's not your afterlife we're concerned with, ma'am. It's your sex life.

Husband: Excuse me?

the inflatable butch

Christopher: Just how satisfying are your sex lives?

Husband: Well, we have been kind of busy lately. Work, the kids, the lawn.

Wife: And Frank's only a man. He'll never *really* understand a woman's needs.

Christopher: Exactly. That's where we'd like to help. Please accept our free publications.

Wife: *The Watchtower*?

Christopher: No, *The Witchtower* for you, and for your husband, *The Bitchtower*. You'll appreciate the humor better once you enter "the life."

Husband: Sorry, but this isn't for us. Things may not be perfect, but the two of us are really quite straight. Now, good-bye.

Louise: But how do you know homosexuality isn't for you until you've tried it?

Husband: Look, friends, we're registered Democrats, we recycle our newspapers, we have a gay nephew. What more do you want?

Louise: We want you to closely examine your hearts and consider all that homosexuality can provide.

the inflatable butch

Now shall we read together on page 4?

Wife: No! For goodness sake, what do we have to do to get you people to leave?

Christopher: Become gay.

Husband: I had a bisexual experience in college. Does that count?

Louise: Only if you write a short story about it.

Christopher: Or produce an independent film.

Wife: Please, it's getting late. The kids are hungry. I must ask you to go.

Louise: All right, but only after we recite the 132 undeniable advantages of a homosexual lifestyle. Number one...

Wife [*throwing her hands in the air*]: All right! You win. We'll do it. Kids, turn off the TV and come here. Your father and I are becoming homosexuals. I'm moving to the East Village to become a performance artist. Frank?

Husband: Well, I've always wanted to run a bed and breakfast. Is Key West still a good spot?

Christopher: Perfect.

Wife: OK, kids, who do you want to go with?

Son: Moving to the city would be totally awesome.

Daughter: I've always wanted to live near the ocean!

Wife: Good, that's settled. I'll cancel the PTA meeting.

Husband: And I'll cancel the bowling league party.

Wife: Think I could have your oxyacetylene blowtorch?

Husband: Sure, honey, if I can have the Dutch oven and Cuisinart.

Wife: You know, I think this is going to work out just fine.

Mission accomplished, Christopher and Louise move on.

JeHomo's Witnesses: Changing lives for the better, one couple at time.

Whatever Gets You Through the Night

Ah, those last, lonely nights of winter. Will you survive them?

Back in December, the long nights didn't phase you: You lit candles, drank ginger tea, and soaked in hot baths filled with holistic mineral oils. Yes, you were quite spiritual about the whole thing.

But now you're over it. You're tired of soggy tea bags, candle stumps, and scrubbing the tub. But most of all, you're sick and tired of hanging out in your apartment, which seems to have shrunk to half its original size. Still, there you are, nonetheless. It's Saturday night; you're disappointed with TV reruns, too tired to get a video, too unmotivated to read. You should just crawl into bed. But that thought is the most depressing of all.

the inflatable butch

Rummaging through your mental list of self-help techniques, you think, *I know! I'll call someone.* Human contact, you recall, is essential for emotional health.

Well, as a public service, let me tell you: Calling around for emotional support on a Saturday night is an exceptionally dumb idea. Think about it. What would happen if you actually picked up that phone and dialed? You'd get an answering machine. Of course.

Yes, that's right. You'd get a chipper, prerecorded voice. It won't tell you the whereabouts of your pals-who-are-always-supposed-to-be-there, but you'd know. You just would.

Your best friend Alicia is on a romantic date with her lover of 14 years. Your second best friend Brandi is at the women's basketball game (she has season tickets, the dog), and your third best friend Claire, whom you don't even like that much, is at a snooty upscale art opening.

You even think of calling your ex-lover, Dory, even though you swore you'd never do that when you're depressed. But you'd get her voice-mail too. You're pretty sure she's at a big noisy party with a hot tub and lots of half-dressed women.

Or wait. Maybe they aren't out at all. Maybe they're all home, screening their calls. In fact, you know they are. Alicia and her lover are just finishing a romantic, home-cooked meal; Brandi has invited friends over for an evening of stimulating

the inflatable butch

conversation; and Claire—she's not at any art opening—she's curled up contentedly with a glass of overpriced liqueur and an intellectual thriller. She's always been so good at taking care of herself, damn it.

And Dory? You're sure she brought home one of those half-dressed women from the hot tub party, and they're now giving each other tantric massages.

OK, so maybe if you actually dialed, you wouldn't be screened through their answering machines. No—worse yet—you'd get a busy signal.

That's right. Alicia's lover is away at a spirituality conference, but that's OK because Alicia is chatting happily with her best friend three towns over. (A best friend who's always there for her, unlike *some* people.)

And Brandi and her evening of stimulating conversation? Well, the bunch of them have gone online to a male chat room. Posing as a set of gay male triplets, Bob, Todd, Rod (each better endowed than the last), they're busy teasing the boys.

Meanwhile, Claire has set aside the book and is presently engaged in phone sex with a woman she met at an improvisational dance concert.

And Dory? Well, that massage just got a little wilder, and her latest playmate, in a moment of flailing ecstasy, knocked the phone off the hook. Neither noticed.

OK, OK. Maybe none of that is true. Maybe if you dialed the phone someone would answer.

But is that what you want? Do you really want to

hear Alicia's happy voice go monotone when she hears it's depressed and despondent you? Will listening to Brandi's gender-bending cyber-exploits about virtual penis-piercing really cheer you up? And I'm sure it would be positively uplifting for you to hear Claire's warm and sultry "hello"—with its sexual hangover informing each syllable. Not that it would be as crushing as a brief, distracted conversation with Dory—giggling and toe-sucking clearly audible throughout.

But, of course, this is pure speculation. It is possible that if you called, one of these women might be home—alone—on a Saturday night. She might, in fact, be as bored, lonely, and depressed as you. In fact, she might be even *more* bored, lonely, and depressed than you.

In that case, why on earth would you want to talk to *her*?

Cough, Sneeze, Hack, Hack

Once upon a time, having a cold was a straight-forward thing. You went to bed for a couple of days, drank orange juice, and, if Jewish, ate chicken soup.

Not anymore. For instance, last month when I felt a sore throat coming on, could I just take two Vitamin C's and go to bed early? No way. Instead, I had to examine *why* I was getting sick. A holistic friend questioned me, "Have you been stressed out, not getting enough sleep, eating poorly?"

"Yes, yes, and yes."

"Then talk to your body. Tell it that you will slow down, get more sleep, and eat healthy foods. Tell your body it doesn't have to get sick in order to make you take care of yourself."

Great. I already have to negotiate with my co-workers, my parents, and my lover. Now I have to negotiate with my cold.

the inflatable butch

But I called in sick for work and canceled my classes. I told my body I'd gotten the message, that I'd take it easy, that these sniffles did not have to develop into a full-fledged cold.

I got sick anyway.

In some ways it was a relief. I now felt legitimate lying around, drinking prepackaged soup, watching reruns of *The Simpsons*. Still, the big question loomed: Now that I'm sick, how do I make myself better?

While there is no cure for the common cold, there's plenty of advice for easing the symptoms. Legions of cold-fighting medicines fill drugstore shelves: pills, liquids, and effervescing tablets, as well as "caplets" and "gel caps." (Who names these things anyway?)

But since I'm a natural kind of gal, I favor natural remedies—not that this simplifies things. For example, to rev up my immune system, I was told to (choose one or more):

(a) brew fresh ginger tea with lemon.
(b) boil an onion in water then drink the water—and eat the onion.
(c) drink miso soup with seaweed.
(d) drip echinacea tincture down my throat.
(e) drink a gallon of water each day to "flush out" my system.

In addition, I was to suck on zinc tablets, swallow

the inflatable butch

Chinese herbs, gargle with warm salt water, run the humidifier, and eat as much garlic as I could stand.

I also took homeopathic remedies. For those of you unfamiliar with homeopathy, this meant that instead of choking down pills, I melted them under my tongue. The directions for this particular homeopathic drug said to take it hourly, making sure your mouth is in its "natural state."

Now before you begin generating explicit images of what your mouth's "natural state" is, the term simply means "don't put anything (yes, anything) in your mouth for 20 minutes before and after melting the pellets under your tongue."

By my calculations, this meant I had one 20-minute period each hour in which to guzzle down my miso soup, orange juice, tall glass of filtered water, and ginger tea, not to mention brush my teeth. Next I had to refrain from all consumption, let my mouth return to its natural state, then ingest the homeopathic remedy, *then* let another 20 minutes pass, mouth unencumbered, before drinking again. It was easy to ignore the beverages during the second 20-minute period as I spent most of it in the bathroom, peeing out all my natural remedies.

As long as I am discussing peeing, I might as well bring up that other prominent bodily function—blowing one's nose.

As I said earlier, I generally ignore commercial products. However, when I am sneezing, sniffling, and dripping, I make an exception. So forget DVDs and

cell phones, I think the greatest invention of the second half of the 20th century is Puffs Plus—the tissue with lotion in it.

And no, I don't want to know the chemical makeup of the lotion, how it gets there, or why it doesn't all ooze to the bottom of the box. I'm sure I could find out if I called my reference librarian friend (who once researched for a fifth-grade boy the average length of a whale penis), but frankly I'd rather be left alone to blow in peace.

So hand me my water glass, pass the Puffs—and, oh, yes, God bless you.

Girlfriend or Vibrator? You Decide!

The sexiest thing happening in my house these days? A naked woman in my shower. Unfortunately, she's only a two-dimensional drawing on my monthly breast exam reminder card.

Yes, things are slow as I find myself once more between relationships, asking myself the most fundamental of questions: What is it that I really need in life—a girlfriend or a vibrator?

It's a complex question, certainly, as both have clear benefits and drawbacks.

Take the vibrator, for instance. Unlike a human, a vibrator is never too tired for sex, is agreeable to a variety of positions, and is pretty much guaranteed not to cheat on you. A vibrator won't steal the covers at night, set her alarm for some ungodly hour, or toss

and turn trying to fall asleep. Also, come daylight, she's happy enough to live under the bed. (Power outages? Now, when the electricity goes out at night, it's a human I want in my bed. Unless, of course, we're talking battery-powered vibrator. In that case, it's a toss-up.)

Of course, relationships are about more than sex and convenience. For instance, one thing I really want in a relationship is a good listener. Naturally, for this need, I turn to my vibrator, as she is remarkably attentive and rarely interrupts.

Still, there are times when technology falls short. Romantic dinners out, for example. Sure, you can put a cute little bow tie on your vibrator, but when you get to the restaurant, she won't eat much, has little to talk about, and always insists on sitting near an outlet. Not to mention, I feel pretty silly two-stepping with my vibrator, even if we do remember to bring the extension cord. We can never figure out who should lead.

And if you think a night on the town is problematic, just try taking her home to meet the folks!

Not that vibrators are perfect on the home front either. While I appreciate that she doesn't complain about the cleanliness level of the apartment, when it *is* time to do chores—clean the refrigerator or rake the leaves, for example—she's fairly useless. Still, I have to give my vibrator credit—when I wrapped a scrubbie around her head in an experimental attempt to clean the barbecue grill, I got no complaints.

the inflatable butch

If, from all this, you think vibrators are boringly predictable, think again. Last month I came home in the middle of the day to find my vibrator logged onto the Internet. Walking toward my Mac, I heard frantic keyboarding and mouse clicks. As I neared the screen, it appeared she'd only been reading posts from a small-appliance newsgroup. But as I did a little more checking, I discovered that she'd spent the last four hours in a sex-toy chat room! I have yet to decide whether she was being unfaithful or just looking for emotional support. And, of course, she won't talk about it.

It's this lack of communication that is the single, biggest mark against vibrators (not that some of my girlfriends have been much better). While I can tolerate that vibrators are poor snuggle partners, make a lousy cup of coffee, and have no clothes you can borrow, without the ability to share and process our feelings, I'm afraid I just couldn't make a long-term commitment to my mechanical friend. And—with no long-term commitment—there's no hope of a commitment ceremony. Sigh.

Not that it's really my vibrator's fault. Because if I look deep down inside myself, I have to confess my own infidelity. How can I make a lifelong pledge when in my heart I know sooner or later I'll be dropping my beloved for a newer model?

Play With Your Words

When I was a kid, my family engaged in many a word game—Scrabble, Boggle, anagrams. But sometimes, when the intellectual element wore thin, we'd break out *Mad Libs*, an oddly compelling form of juvenile entertainment in which we supplied missing words to a story. Thirty years later, I've decided to write my own version, which in a rare burst of non-creativity I have dubbed *Lesbian Libs*.

But before we start, a quick grammar lesson for everyone who spent English class daydreaming about the girl sitting next to you, the girl sitting in front of you, or if you were one of the brave ones, the teacher herself.

So just what is a noun? A noun is a person, place, or thing. *Janet Reno, moon, porcupine*—these are all nouns. An adjective describes a noun, i.e., *hefty, dreary*, or *shocking pink*. Verbs are action

the inflatable butch

words, such as *run*, *laugh*, *cough*, or *process*. Those are the basics. For the not so basic, find a grammar geek. Chances are, she'll be happy to tell you all about it.

To play this game, you need two or more people. (That's right, this is real game. Go ahead, God won't strike you down for writing in a book. Besides, it's only a paperback.) OK, so the leader (or facilitator, depending on your social circle) asks the others to supply nouns, verbs, and adjectives without reading the surrounding text. She fills in the blanks, then once she's finished, reads the brilliantly sardonic piece aloud.

So set aside your grammarphobia and get ready to play!

THE GAME

As I sat at the <u>field hockey</u> (name of sport) game, my eyes wandered <u>3</u> (number) rows down to a woman with <u>maroon</u> (color) hair and a <u>silky</u> (adjective) jacket. Immediately obsessed, I walked down and sat in the seat next to her.

"<u>I luv yo</u> (salutation) *doin*," I said. "I couldn't help notice

the inflatable
butch

your __warm__ jacket. Is it from __India__?"
     (adjective)   (name of country)

"No, I bought it in __Arkansas__."
                    (U.S. state)

"Say, the game is getting a little __smooth__.
                                    (adjective)

Would you like to grab a __apple juice__ and __stepping__?"
                          (liquid)   (verb)

"That sounds __quiet__," she said. "My name
             (adjective)

is __~~Jamie~~ Maggie__"
   (name of woman in the room)

"I'm __~~Kirsten~~ ~~Tammy~~ Glen__," she said
      (name of another woman in the room)

as she shook my __stomach__.
                (body part)

We got into my __glossy__ __volvo__ and headed
               (adjective) (type of car)

to my favorite café, __2__ __Peaches__.
                     (number) (plural noun)

Over our drinks, we spoke briefly of __cushy__
                                     (adjective)

__sheets__, __bright__ __sleeping bags__, and
(plural noun) (adjective) (plural noun)

__dark__ __cell phone__
(adjective) (plural noun)

Then I suddenly felt shy, until she said, "I imagine

80   **ellen orleans**

the inflatable butch

that your __hips__ is very __open__."
    (body part)   (adjective)

"Would you like to find out?" I asked. "My apartment is only __6__ blocks away."
                                              (number)

Less than __13__ minutes later, with
         (number)

__bras, panties, belt__ strewn about, we lay
(three articles of clothing)

wiggling on the __ottoman__.
                (piece of furniture)

"__Whoa baby__! Do that again!" she cried out.
 (exclamation)

"You mean put my __back__ on your __neck__?"
                 (body part)   (body part)

"No, on my __head__."
           (body part)

I did, and she cried out, "__Damn__! I haven't
                           (exclamation)

I haven't been this excited since __Arbor Day__."
                                    (holiday)

"Oh, __Sweet pea__," I said, "you're an
     (term of endearment)

absolute __elephant__."
         (kind of animal)

A few minutes later...
I snuggled contentedly next to __Kristen__, Ta Glen
                                (name of second woman)

ellen orleans

the inflatable butch

<u> Cool </u> waves of tenderness spreading over me.
(adjective)

"I love you," I cooed. "Come live with me, and we'll be happy for <u> 8 </u> <u> Months </u>."
                                 (number) (measure of time)

"Uh-oh," she said. "There's something I should tell you. I have a husband and two <u> skirts </u>."
                                                   (plural noun)

GOING TO THE PRIDE PARADE

Last month I went to my very first pride parade, which is a big deal since I've only been out for _____ _____.
(number) (measure of time)
The parade was led by Dykes on _____,
(mode of transportation)
which was very exciting, especially when one of them with _____
(adjective)
hair and _____ leather boots waved her _____
(color)   (body part)
at me.

The group that got the most applause was Parents and Friends of _____ and _____.
                                  (plural noun)   (plural noun)

the inflatable butch

They held signs that said, I LOVE MY GAY _____
(noun)

and MY _____ DAUGHTER IS FINE JUST THE WAY
(adjective)

SHE IS! I was so touched that I began to _____.
(verb)

My favorite part was when Queer Nation marched by and chanted, "We're _____, we're
(adjective)
_____, get used to it!"
(adjective)

After the parade there was lots of stuff to buy. I got a rainbow _____ and a rainbow
(item of clothing)
_____ and a T-shirt that says NOBODY
(household appliance)
KNOWS I'M A _____.
(noun)

The big surprise came when a very famous person came out. I never knew _____
(famous man who is still alive)
was really a lesbian!

COUPLES COUNSELING

My girlfriend _____ and I
(name of woman in the room)

the inflatable
butch

sat on a long beige _____. I felt very
(piece of furniture)

_____.
(adjective describing a feeling)

"So," Dr. _____ said,
(last name of famous person)

"You've been together for _____ _____
(number)   (measure of time)

now?"

"That's right," _____ said, "but we
(name of first woman)

were_____ together for _____
(verb ending in "ing")   (number)

_____ before that."
(measure of time)

"And now you two are feeling _____?"
(adjective)

My girlfriend glared at me. "Only after she

started _____ with _____."
(verb ending in "ing")   (name)

The doctor looked at me. "Is this true?"

"Yes," I said, "but I swear it only happened

_____ times."
(number greater than one)

The doctor looked at my girlfriend. "And how
did that make you feel?"

the inflatable butch

"_____. I wanted to throw all her
 (adjective)

_____ out of the _____."
(plural noun)   (noun)

"But I said I was sorry," I told her, "and I brought you a bouquet of _____ and a box
(plural noun)

of _____. And besides, you'd been spending all
 (food)

that time with _____ at the _____."
              (woman's name)   (location)

"I only did that because you said to get in touch with my inner _____."
                                (noun)

"Well, you insisted on that spiritual _____
                                      (exercise)

class, 'Heal Your _____.'"
                   (noun)

"Only after you dragged us to the Conscious _____ workshop."
(emotion)

"Now, now," our therapist said. "Blaming each other is never _____. Tell me, what are your
              (adjective)

interests?"

"Well," my girlfriend began, "I like

ellen orleans

the inflatable
butch

_____, _____, and
(verb ending in "ing")   (verb ending in "ing")

_____."
(plural noun)

"And I enjoy _____ and
                    (verb ending in "ing")

_____. And we both like to _____."
(plural noun)   (verb)

"Well, that's a start," the doctor said. "Now, tell me, how is your _____ life?"
                                                                   (activity)

"_____," we both sighed.
(adjective)

"Have you considered making a special date for _____? It would be a _____
                                                (verb ending in "ing")   (adjective)

opportunity to work on your _____
                              (verb ending in "ing")

skills. Can you make a commitment to that? Perhaps once a _____?"
                                                          (measure of time)

My girlfriend and I looked at each other. "That sounds pretty _____," she said.
                                                              (adjective)

I shook my head. "I don't know. Maybe we should have a _____ instead."
                                                        (noun)

ellen orleans

Go With the (Cash) Flow

Lately it seems I've been surrounded by financially savvy dykes. But after hours of drowning in money talk—dividing it, saving it, spending it—I want to get down to the real question: Is it better to have a girlfriend who has more money than you or less money than you?

At first glance, more seems better. But is it? Sure, it's nice to have that built-in Jacuzzi and 48-inch high-definition TV, but in turn you have to live up to her buying power. It's a drag to always be the one saying, "Let's choose the cheaper seats at the Joan Armatrading concert." Or "No, I can't afford dinner at Chez Léz. How about the Rusty Radish instead?" Of course, she can treat, if you don't mind feeling ten years old.

OK, so what about the alternative? Let's say you're the one with the dough. But as sugar mama,

the inflatable butch

you're now tied down to that dull-as-dirt tech-writing job just so you can pay your proportionally correct share of the rent. You give up your little luxuries in order for things to feel balanced. After all, how can you feast on fresh salmon while she eats canned tuna?

But when you think about it, this money thing isn't really about amounts—it's about attitudes. I learned this one day when I came home to find my girlfriend practically in tears.

"What's wrong?" I asked, lovingly putting my arm around her shoulder.

"I bounced a check," she told me.

"And?" I asked, removing my arm. Clearly, this was not the emotional crisis I'd imagined. "What happened? Did an airline reservation fall through because of it? Do you have $100 in bank fees?"

"No, it's just that I've never bounced a check before. I feel so humiliated."

"Humiliation?" I repeated. "Babe, I got over that 90 bounced checks ago." Then, helpful as ever, I explained my five-step program for returned checks:

1. You spend a lengthy three seconds acknowledging your part in it, as in depositing not enough money too late into the wrong account.
2. You curse the bank for not covering the $1.06 difference between bouncing and clearing.

the inflatable butch

3. You curse the $20 returned-check fee.
4. You curse capitalism in general.
5. You get on with your life.

My exegesis complete, my girlfriend just stared at me—clearly overcome with admiration and gratitude. This made me realize that along with being able to discuss sex, levels of visibility, and animal allergies, it was essential that we—and all couples—be able to talk about money.

To that end, I have supplied this heavily researched, psychologically sophisticated money quiz for you and your sweetheart to take together. Be sure to leave plenty of time to process.

1. Financial stability is:
   (a) my IRA, to which I contribute $2,400 annually.
   (b) random investments in socially conscious companies.
   (c) a $30 buffer in my checking account.
   (d) that big jar of loose change I keep near the fish tank.

2. A joint checking account is:
   (a) a practical way to pay household expenses.
   (b) a political statement to our local bank.
   (c) a testimony to our love and commitment.
   (d) more likely to end our relationship than a tawdry affair.

the inflatable butch

3. I only use credit cards when I:
   (a) have to book an emergency flight home for a funeral.
   (b) have left my cash and checkbook at home 25 miles away.
   (c) have left my cash and checkbook in the car 25 feet away.
   (d) am sure that a pair of $300 snakeskin boots will make me happy forever.

4. I prefer to:
   (a) be neurotically aware of my every last penny but debt-free.
   (b) be in massive denial about the state of my finances, yet at peace with the world.
   (c) wear ratty, stained T-shirts, despite my $90,000-a-year trust fund.
   (d) buy $80 preripped jeans, even if it means surviving on generic ramen noodles for the next three weeks.

5. Which of the following maxims best describes your attitude toward money?
   (a) A penny saved is a penny earned.
   (b) Live simply so that others may simply live.
   (c) Do what you love; the money will follow.
   (d) Jesus saves; Moses invests.

Clearly, there are no right answers in this quiz. Its purpose instead is to prompt honest discussion

about money between you and your partner. So go on, take her and this quiz to the nearest espresso bar, buy a couple of heavily caffeinated beverages, and start talking. And by the way, let her treat.

On the Road—Lesbian Style

Last month I took off for my world-class whirlwind book tour of...the Midwest. Now, while people make fun of the Midwest, I often find my best audiences there. Midwesterners, unlike cynical big-city types, aren't afraid to laugh. This is a big plus for us humor writers. Besides, you never know what you'll learn on a road trip.

DAY 1: DEPARTURE

With items vital to my trip newly purchased—sneakers, blue jeans, and a watch—I am ready for my journey. Oh, yeah, I throw in the books I'll need for my readings plus a few maps. I've also got a key to my friend Karin's place in Lincoln, where I'll be spending the night. Karin cautions me not to be shocked—a Xena shrine dominates her apartment. Duly forewarned, I head out, only four hours behind schedule.

the inflatable butch

Colorado's a big state. I drive for hours before I reach Sterling, where I stop for dinner. There, a vegetarian sandwich means they dump all their toppings into a roll. I order one anyway.

Nebraska is a long state. Real long. But by 1 A.M. I'm unlocking the door to my friend's apartment. It does not, as she said, *contain* a Xena shrine; it *is* a Xena shrine. Lucy Lawless grimaces at me from all directions. Gabrielle is more welcoming. I fall asleep immediately.

DAY 2: IOWA, MOSTLY

Iowa is not quite as long, but there are more trucks to contend with. To quell my boredom with I-80, I try out a book on tape: *Do What You Love, The Money Will Follow*. *Yes*, I think, listening, *but are we talking thick wads of cash following in a Cadillac or a roll of dimes on a skateboard, scurrying to catch up?*

DAY 3: CHICAGO

As I emerge from my basement bedroom in my brother's house, my 22-month-old niece, Leah, spots me. It's been six weeks since she's seen me, but she remembers me. You see, during my last visit, as I, fully dressed, watched her play in the tub, she graciously included me in the fun by dousing me with a cup of water. Today she sees me and exclaims, "Aunt Ellen, pour water on head!" I'm touched by my new appellation.

the inflatable butch

That night I read at People Like Us bookstore. Turnout is small, but after my reading, a woman in the audience asks me how I integrate my spirituality into my writing. I find myself talking about Hebrew school and other childhood traumas with a bunch of strangers. These kind of unexpected heart-to-hearts are what readings are all about.

DAY 4: THE VOWEL STATES

After leaving Illinois, I hit Indiana, where one town announces itself "The Manufactured Housing and Recreational Vehicle Capital of the World." Now there's something to crow about. Around 6 P.M. I drop off I-80, heading south toward my college reunion. A sign outside a church reads HEAVEN: DON'T MISS IT FOR THE WORLD. I'll try to keep that in mind.

I'd had qualms about this reunion. *What's the point*, I wonder? But as soon as I reach the outskirts of town, I know this is exactly where I am supposed to be. I am not here to simply see old friends. I am here to meet up with my past.

DAY 5 THROUGH 7: OHIO

I'm having a great time. At 1 A.M. I'm still sitting on the dorm lounge floor, talking with people I haven't spoken to in years. We laugh that we're not really 18 again and don't really have the stamina to be up till 1 in the morning. Then we stay up talking till 2.

Why is this reunion so much better than the one ten years ago? Simple. I am out. And on Saturday night, I take my "outness" one step further. I'm part of Entertainment Night, and in front of 100 old classmates I take the stage and address them.

"Now it's no secret that I'm a lesbian—*now*," I begin. "But while I was in school here, I hadn't figured that out yet. I tried really hard, or at least pretty hard, to be heterosexual. I was brave and asked men out. Trouble was, I always asked out gay men. As you can imagine, things never went very far. During my first month here, I swear, every single person in my dorm was having sex. Except me. Up and down the hall, everyone losing his or her virginity. Like it was a distribution requirement.

"But that's long since past. Now, 14 years later, I return to reclaim my sexuality. And to that end, I am going to read for you the sex scene from my book, *The Butches of Madison County*."

And so I did. It was very, as they say, empowering.

DAY 8: MICHIGAN
(NO, NOT *THAT* MICHIGAN)

The day after my class reunion ends, I resume my book tour. I'm off to A Woman's Prerogative in Ferndale, where the store's owner, Kelly, has set up a reading. As usual, I try unsuccessfully to follow my map and scribbled directions while hurtling down the highway at 70 mph. Thus it's no surprise that three hours later I am lost on the outskirts of Detroit,

driving the only non-American car in a 300-block radius.

Eventually, though, I make my way to Nine Mile Road, where the store is supposed to be. But I find no store. I do, however, spot a truck plastered with feminist bumper stickers in front of a house with a rainbow flag. Figuring the store is located in the house, I walk to the door. A woman answers. "I'm looking for Kelly," I say.

Without missing a beat, she replies, "Oh, you're looking for the bookstore. You want *West* Nine Mile Road; this is *East* Nine Mile." She then gives me exemplary directions.

Wow! How does she know I want the bookstore? Do I have DYKE AUTHOR, BAD WITH DIRECTIONS stamped on my forehead? Does this woman greet lost lesbian bibliophiles at her door every day? I never find out her name, but to this fine Sapphist shepherd, I offer my thanks.

The Tuesday night reading in Ferndale goes well, finishing up just in time for the 8:30 softball game.

DAY 9 AND 10: MICHIGAN AND ILLINOIS

I read at Common Language in Ann Arbor, where the Ph.D.s in the audience are pleased with the scientific accuracy of my essay on gay DNA. The next day, I snake down the back roads to Once Upon a Time books in Bloomington/Normal.

In addition to books, this place has the most

the inflatable butch

amazing collection of gay and lesbian sidelines I've ever seen: PFLAG greeting cards, queer mousepads, rainbow jockey shorts, and piles more. "You must really draw in the college crowd with all this," I say to the owner, Tana, whose girlfriend turns out to be an ex-lover of a friend of mine back home. (Neither of us is particularly surprised.)

"Oh, we don't get much business from the university," she replies.

"Why not?"

"People are afraid to come into the store."

"Why? This seems like a safe part of town."

She looks at me as if I'm from another planet. "They're afraid to be branded as gay."

I can't believe it. "Oh, for Pete's sake, it's not like this store is a radical leftist commune."

"This is farm country," she explains. "Conservative farm country. Gay people lose their jobs, their students, their houses."

Wow.

Thus sobered up, that night I read to a small but highly appreciative crowd, amazed once again at how far our struggle has yet to go.

Day 11: (More or Less) Iowa

My drive home on Route 80 takes me back through Iowa, where I realize I'll soon be driving directly north of Madison County. I can't resist. I have to see those bridges. I swing down 281, then east on 92. But outside of Indianola there's a detour,

which puts me north onto 69 and down through Cumming and then...I'm lost.

Driving southwest along an unnamed diagonal gray strip on the map, the irony finally dawns on me. Just like Robert in the *Bridges of Madison County*, just like Billie in the *Butches of Madison County*, I am lost. Yes, I've become yet another character: Ellen in the *Detours of Madison County*. Thus the question remains: Will I find a young, comely farmwife to provide me with both directions *and* a torrid love affair?

No such luck. Instead of a farmwife, I find a sign to Cedar Bridge. Driving through the covered bridge, I park my car in the deserted lot and walk back. It is a lonely place, reeking of broken heterosexual hearts. I go back to my car, open the trunk, and pull out a copy of *Butches*. On the inside cover I write:

For those of us who love
in a slightly different way.

I walk back to the bridge, give the book a queer blessing, tuck it in a crevice. *Will anyone find it?* I wonder. *Will it change a life?*

Driving slowly back through, I shake my head at my authorial act of defiance. We all spread freedom in different ways, I suppose.

I then take off, heading west, heading home.

Sensible Shoes, Practical Pussy

There's an odd phenomenon afoot. While women's bars are closing down in the real world, they are popping up all over movie and TV screens. Hollywood's version of dyke dance clubs baffles me, though, as they are filled with women who don't look like any lesbians I know.

I think it's the clothes. In these fictional clubs, the outfits drip with attitude. The women wear low-cut polyester blouses that tease, pinstripe miniskirts that intimidate, retro accessories that gloat. Their clothes always have something to say: "Let's dance like sluts. Let's initiate a hostile takeover. Let's debate submerged lesbian content in a noncontextual academic setting." Or simply: "Do me."

Watching these Hollywood versions of lesbian

the inflatable butch

culture, I glance at my own clothes. The only thing they say is "Hey! Want to go hiking?"

It's true. Fashion-wise, my clothes rarely get past the sneakers, jeans, and button-down shirt stage. Recently, to counter my dull image, I tried to be daring. I donned a black shirt, tasteful plaid blazer, and tan boots. Sure, I made a fashion statement—I looked like Jewish mafia.

Sadly enough, what's true in Hollywood does have bearing in the noncelluloid world. Case in point: Before it metamorphosed into yet another boring straight bar, I visited Denver's girl club, The Elle. I hadn't been there in years, so while boogying away on the dance floor, I was surprised to behold "The Elle Dancers."

Standing on raised platforms amid the rest of us, these skinny young women gyrated to the pulsing beat, bedecked in gold lamé bras, black sequined skirts, and red stiletto pumps. They twirled necklaces, moved their hips suggestively, even got down and pressed groin to floor. While the club patrons cheered them on—wild fantasies undoubtedly rolling about in their heads—the only thought going through my mind was, *Those clothes can't be very comfortable.*

Alas, it's true—their raw sexuality did nothing for me. As I continued to bop and spin, I wondered, what kind of Elle dancer *would* rock my world?

Meet Lou Ann, lumberyard saleswoman. Dressed in heavy denim and a blue workshirt, she

stands solid on her dance block, simply tapping her steel-toed boot to the beat. Getting funky, she pulls a tape measure from her leather utility belt and tosses it from hand to hand. She throws me a smile, and I'm in sawdust heaven.

Then there's Carmen, computer geek. Wearing a leather belt studded with Pentium processor chips, she whispers URL addresses and HTML code while suggestively entangling and disentangling herself in a shiny blue Ethernet cable. It's bi-directional. After a few minutes, I'm begging this sweet thing to plug into my ports.

And who can resist Gaia, gardening goddess? Baby-blue overalls streaked with organic dirt cover the voluptuous body of this sensuous babe. Hand trowel in one pocket, crocus bulbs in another, in a fit of unbridled sensuality she tosses a fistful of marigold seeds in my direction.

Finally, Nerd Girl. And I don't mean retro Nerd Girl either. No make-a-statement, thick-framed eyeglasses or 1950s suburban-husband pocket shirts for her. I mean *authentic* Nerd Girl, with unstylish wire-rimmed specs, a T-shirt that never heard the word *chic*, and blue jeans she inherited from a former roommate.

Authentic Nerd Girl jumps off her dancing block, and together we abandon the bar for an unassuming diner where she and I sit in the nonsmoking section, consuming vegetarian food and decaf beverages. For the next three hours, we talk about snowshoe trails,

women writers, meatless recipes, and a variety of spiritual practices. Of course, being a nerd girl myself, I find this more titillating than a whole mountain of lace bras and leather miniskirts.

For our first official date, we go on a moonlight hike. After all, we're both already dressed for it.

Minding Your Matrimonial Manners

This September, I had the pleasure of attending my first lover's commitment ceremony. During the second half of the Quaker-style service, guests were invited share their thoughts and good wishes with Lori and Martha, the radiant couple in question.

I began my short speech thus: "According to the Homosexual Rule Book, every lesbian wedding must include at least one ex-lover. I'm happy to say that I fulfill that particular obligation here today." Then, as I am a psychologically evolved former girlfriend, I went on to give my blessings to the two of them.

It later occurred to me that since not all my readers are as well-adjusted as I, it is nothing less than my civic duty to help all of you navigate the weddings of your own ex-lovers—this the most trying of social

occasions. So whether you are a bridesmaid, best gal, *chuppah* holder, or mere guest, here's a chance to brush up on your queer nuptials etiquette. Just follow these simple (and chronological) steps and you'll be avoiding those embarrassing matrimonial-related faux pas in no time.

1. Finding Out: If, upon receiving the invitation, your immediate reaction is to shred it, along with the reply card, directions, and inner and outer envelopes, consider declining the invitation altogether.

2. Prewedding Planning: Don't wear that custom-made T-shirt emblazoned with an enlarged image of you and your former honey together, naked and muddy, at Michigan. Similarly, avoid wearing your FUCK MONOGAMY baseball cap.

3. Preceremony Socializing: Comments about your ex, such as "I guess she finally ended that affair with the dyke contractor," are not helpful.

While I'm sure you have the best of intentions, it's nonetheless more courteous to stick to such topics as recent movies and household pets than to remark to the guests, "Hey, there's Rosa Boomstaff, our old couples counselor. I hope my ex and her new babe have more luck in therapy than we did!"

4. Ceremony Basics: As she walks down the aisle, do not call out, "Hey, didn't you wear that

same dress during our 'Buffy and Willow' fantasy party two years ago?" And even if your ex did dump you on Valentine's Day, it's still not OK to bring your sluttiest friend to the ceremony and make out in the second row. Save this behavior for the dance floor.

If you are asked to say something spiritual during the ceremony, don't begin with the words "Gosh, honey, I guess this means it's really over between us." If you find yourself sitting directly behind another of her exes, restrain yourself from comparing notes. Do this (discreetly) at the reception.

5. In the Buffet Line: Do not comment, "That dip looks just like the lentil paté she and I spread over each other's nipples that weekend in Taos."

6. At the Reception: It is poor taste to say to the couple's officiating minister, "I guess our lovely bride will be resigning from the Polyamorous Pagans Society." It is acceptable, however, to flirt with the above-stated minister, especially if you and she are of the same denomination.

When the music starts and the new couple walks toward the dance floor, don't yell out, "Hey, that was our song!" You may, however, quietly sulk in a corner.

Don't hit on the new bride. Either of them. Or their mothers. You can, however, try your luck with any unattached sisters, aunts, or cousins.

7. Gifts: Remember those six CDs you swiped from her the day she moved out to be with her new honey? No, you cannot now wrap them up as gifts. Also, unless your relationship ended years ago and you two are really, really good friends, multiple-attachment vibrators are not appropriate. But if you do decide to go that route, remember to get one in her favorite color.

8. Finally: It is always considered bad manners to whisper to her new partner, "Trust me, babe, you'll never be butch enough for her."

Barbie, Ben, and Me

Last August, while spending time with my six-year-old nephew Ben, I asked him what he wanted for his upcoming birthday.

"A Barbie," he told me. "But send it for Christmas, not my birthday."

"Why?" I asked. "Your birthday comes before Christmas."

"I don't want the other kids to see it when I unwrap my presents."

Now, this was interesting. Not only did Ben want a "nontraditional" toy, but he also knew he'd better keep it a secret. So much for progress in gender equality. Still, I thought it was cool Ben had the guts to ask for a Barbie at all.

I decided to talk to my sister-in-law Sue, Ben's mom, about it. "I was asking Ben what he wanted for his birthday and—"

the inflatable butch

"He wants a Barbie," she sighed. "I know."

Upon hearing Sue say this, my first lesbian thought was, *Does my sister-in-law think playing with dolls will turn her kid into a sissy? And what's so bad about being a sissy anyway?*

Sue continued. "Of all the dolls, he wants a *Barbie*. Barbie is just so...so unfeminist."

Oh, so *that* was the problem. Ben had a Jasmine doll, along with Aladdin and a bag full of action figures. No one seemed to have issues about that. But I still had nagging doubts about Sue: Did she buy into the idea that playing with dolls makes boys gay?

When I mentioned Ben's Barbie doll request to my own mother, she too was aware of it. Apparently, Ben was not afraid to campaign for what he wanted. "Get him a Skipper doll," she suggested. "Skipper isn't so 'developed.'"

As September rolled around, I found myself obsessing—what did it mean for a boy to want a Barbie? Was it an early clue to impending homosexuality? Or did it more likely mean heterosexuality—what with Ben's fascination with big-breasted Barbie and her 1-inch waist? Or was it some combination of the two pointing to bisexuality?

Then I caught myself. Would I be doing this level of questioning if my niece had asked for a Barbie? No. I would have simply dismissed it as social conditioning and gotten her a nice nonsexist book instead.

So, for better or worse, a week later I found

the inflatable
butch

myself in a huge, impersonal toy store staring at a bright pink wall of Barbies. Let me tell you, it was one rude awakening. What did I know about Barbie? The doll I played with when I was Ben's age was a knight, complete with plastic armor and choice of helmets.

I had no idea there were so many Barbies—so many *white* Barbies, that is—not to mention all her outfits and accessories. There was Wedding Barbie and Roller-Blade Barbie and *Baywatch* Barbie, complete with her own dolphin. There was even a vintage Barbie, a 1960 torch-song crooner with a sequined dress. A good choice for my cross-dresser friends.

I briefly considered a combo pack—Barbie with three outfits: schoolteacher clothes, lab jacket, and a firefighter uniform. (I've always like a doll in uniform.) But then it dawned on me—what Ben liked about Barbie was the frills. If he wanted the tailored look, he'd be content with GI Joe.

But still, as a feminist, I had my doubts. Big doubts. Big immobilizing doubts.

Start with the doll, I told myself, *then figure out the clothes*. I decided to choose from the smaller selection of black Barbies. I thought this was a small victory for nonconformity, although with black Barbie's obviously Caucasian features, who was I kidding?

Then I went to the clothes section. There were all kinds of neat choices—soccer player clothes, a police

uniform, a cowboy outfit. Then I realized that these weren't Barbie's clothes—they were Ken's!

What was a lesbian to do? Was it time to give up and buy a box of Legos? Order a handwoven vest from a Guatemalan cooperative? Run out of the store screaming? No. It was time to get it together, choose something—anything—and *then* run out of the store screaming. I bought Barbie a white satin dress and a cowboy outfit.

Now, I didn't know what supporting Mattel would do to my karma, but at least Ben would know he could depend on his lesbian Aunt Ellen to break gender barriers for him. Also, with my help, he'd be joining a great tradition of children who cross-dress their Barbies.

I took my plunder home and gift-wrapped it, writing "Private! For Ben Only!" on the package. Also, I added a note: "Remember, Ben, in real life women do not have permanently arched feet."

When I told my mother what I'd sent Ben, she seemed concerned about my sister-in-law's reaction, which of course brought up my own worries. Would Sue give me the cold shoulder for aiding and abetting her son's decline into homosexual depravity? Would she shun me for supporting sexist toys?

A couple of weeks later I got a note from Sue. "Great minds think alike," she wrote. "I bought Ben a Dancin' Barbie. He's in heaven."

Here Come the Brides

Ah, the Defense of Marriage Act, alternatively known as the "Gay Marriage is Icky" Act. Finally, something Democrats and Republicans can agree upon.

I'm not sure what upsets them so. The fact that lesbians look better in tuxes than straight guys? As a writer, though, what I most appreciate is the potent images the title "Defense of Marriage Act" conjures up. I can't help visualizing a bewildered Caucasian family huddled together—Mom, Dad, two kids, and a black lab—bravely defending their simple God-fearing marriage from vast hordes of the OTHER!

Picture it: To the east, a battalion of cross-dressers advances toward the humble hetero family; to the west, a regiment of gay male bodybuilders, its members quarreling with each other: "The husband is mine!" "No, I saw him first!" To the south, a lesbian

the inflatable butch

equestrian unit charges over the hill, chanting their battle cry: "Pro-CESS! Pro-CESS!"

Scattered bands of queer skate-punk activists call to the kids, "You can escape your parents' mind-numbingly insipid world! Join us! We'll show you how to stop traffic, jump police barricades, and drink way too much caffeine!"

Finally, the Lesbian Avengers, hiding in the treetops, taunt the besieged husband: "Two-four-six-eight! How do you know your wife is straight?"

Then there's formerly closeted Republican congressman Jim Kolbe. He says he voted for DOMA because he believes each state should be able to define marriage for itself. Now, there's an interesting proposition—each state deciding who can and cannot marry. I wonder how that would work...

Alabama: White people can only marry other white people, and everyone else has to leave the state.

Mississippi: Same-sex couples can marry in Mississippi, but only if they promise to move to Manhattan after tossing the rice.

Massachusetts: Same-sex couples can marry, but only if they are of the same political party.

New Hampshire: Same-sex couples can marry, but only if both are registered Republicans.

Vermont: Same-sex couples can marry, but only if both are registered socialists.

Michigan: Same-sex couples can marry, but only if both drive American cars.

Louisiana: Any kind of couple can marry as long as they bribe the governor.

Utah: No queer marriages, of course, but a man can have as many wives as he wants. What all those women do together in the privacy of their own home, well, that's their business.

And why stop at state rights? Why not let individual cities and, heck, even neighborhoods, decide for themselves?

Hollywood: Members of the same sex can marry as long as both continue to stay in the closet.

San Francisco: Of course, same-sex couples can marry. At this point in time, however, opposite-sex couples can only register as domestic partners. Please be patient and don't complain. Someday you'll have the same rights as everyone else. Really.

The Lesbian Intervention Squad

It's a peaceful evening as Carrie and Bari cuddle up on Carrie's couch. Lovers for three months now, this morning they signed their first lease together. As they bask in the glow of commitment, the phone rings. After a brief conversation, Carrie turns to Bari.

Carrie: That was Marge. She's on her way over. Said it was important.

[*Sharp knock at the door. Marge bustles in.*]

Marge: [*brusquely*] Is that the new lease?

Bari: Uh-huh.

the inflatable butch

[*Marge scoops it up and rips it in half.*]

Carrie and Bari: What are you doing?! Are you nuts?!

Marge: It's for the best. [*Marge nods toward the door.*] Come on in, girls.

[*Jackie and Joan stomp on in.*]

Carrie and Bari: What's going on here?

Marge: This, Carrie and Bari, is a lesbian intervention.

Bari: An intervention? Are you saying we're alcoholics? Coke addicts?

Marge: Worse. You're lesbians moving in too soon. And we are here to prevent it.

Bari: Look, we've thoroughly scrutinized, analyzed, and discussed moving in. We're ready.

Marge: Talk is cheap. Reality is not. Let's hear what your former housemates have to say. Jackie?

Jackie: [*stepping forward*] Carrie, you're an extroverted coffee-drinking morning person who vacuums daily, arranges her shoes by height, and alphabetizes the Lean Cuisines in the freezer.

the inflatable butch

Bari: You do?

Joan: Bari, you're an introverted rice-milk-drinking night owl who owns neither a vacuum nor a mop, rarely returns her phone messages, and lets the cat box sit for weeks.

Bari: I scoop!

Joan: Bari watches PBS; Carrie, FOX.

Jackie: Carrie owns three phones: cellular, speaker, and cordless. Bari owns one: rotary.

Bari: Sure, we have a few differences. We've processed and compensated.

Marge: Oh, really? And have you processed your book situation?

Carrie: Book situation?

Marge: Bari, how many boxes of books do you own?

Bari: Twenty, twenty-five. Thirty at the most.

Marge: Including the ones in my garage?

Carrie: You have books in Marge's garage?

the inflatable butch

Bari: OK, 50. I own 50 boxes of books.

Carrie: Fifty boxes? Where are we going to put them?

Bari: [*curtly*] Same place we're going to put your 80-piece "Goddesses Around the Globe" collection, 20-gallon iguana tank, and double birdcage. [*turning to Marge and the gals*] Anyway, our issues are none of your business.

Jackie: [*stepping forward*] Oh, really? And who's the strongest dyke you know?

Bari: You.

Jackie: And who were you counting on to haul those books up three flights of stairs?

Bari: Uh, you. You know we both have back trouble.

Jackie: And whose truck were you planning to borrow?

Bari: Uh, yours.

Joan: That's right. It's going to be Jackie, Joan, and Marge, packing and hauling. Jackie, Joan, and Marge, pulling muscles, scraping knuckles, schlepping enraged cats across town. And to what avail? So you can live happily ever after? No. So you can spend eight

weeks together, discover how utterly incompatible you are, and break up—calling us in total desperation to pack everything back up and haul it to a new place.

Marge: Frankly, we're not going to let that happen.

Carrie: Well, you're too late. Our landlady already has a signed contract and one month's deposit. It's a done deal.

Marge: Actually, not. I talked to her this afternoon. Here's your lease back, null and void.

Bari: But—but you don't have any say in this.

Marge: Technically, perhaps not. But aside from being a property owner, your landlady is also a couples counselor. When we explained the situation, she immediately canceled the contract. Section 16A, Roman numeral III: Grossly incompatible lovers may not cohabitate, regardless of race, creed, or sexual orientation.

Carrie: But we put down 800 bucks on that place!

Marge: She gave back the deposit. In cash. [*hands over the money*] $400 for Bari; $400 for Carrie.

Bari: [*to Carrie*] Wait a minute. I put down $410; you only put down $390.

Carrie: That's because I treated at dinner the other night.

Bari: But you owe me for the Lean Cuisines I picked up for you.

Marge: Ha! Money issues. Let's not go there.

Bari: But...but we love each other.

Marge: Love, shmove. Be practical, girls. If you're still together in a year and want to move in, we'll reconsider. *[Beep! Beep!]* My pager. Hmm, looks like Bonnie and Connie have decided to have a baby. C'mon, gals, let's go. This squad has work to do.

Bookseller, Bartender, Therapist, Geek

For the last year, I've been working a shift at our local women's bookstore. Now, for those of you who figure this line of work is just one big flirt fest for us lesbian gals, think again. First of all, who can tell who's queer anymore? I try to be smooth and end up making a pass at a PFLAG mom.

So what is a typical day like? Much of it is full of geeky book searches and product codes, leaving little time to be literary. Checking in new inventory is perhaps the most stimulating part—personally, I love seeing what wacky titles the publishers come up with each week. The winner for most inane title goes to *My God! My Child Is Gay!* with the second place bestowed upon *The Idiot's Guide to Adoption*. (Look, it's fine if idiots want to learn Photoshop or

the inflatable butch

do their own taxes, but if you truly consider yourself an idiot, do everyone a favor and adopt a goldfish, not a child.)

But most of all, it's the people that make bookstore life exciting. You see, without them I wouldn't be able to indulge in my favorite work-a-day pastime: "Guess the Customer's Private Life Based on What She Buys." I've got it down to a science:

Loving Someone Gay and six rainbow stickers? Newly out.

Slim volume of poetry and a candle? New girlfriend.

Naiad romance and a tarot deck? New girlfriend gone for the weekend.

Three detective novels, "Dyke Firefighters" calendar, and a large bag of chocolates? Girlfriend gone for good.

On Our Backs and massage oil? Next girlfriend.

These customers are the easy ones. They know what they want, they buy it, and they go home. It's the lost souls who are the real challenge. Over the months, I've finally learned they don't want to buy anything; they just want someone to talk to. Helping them is like being a bartender, except you don't get tips—like being a therapist, except you make $8 and not $80 an hour.

For instance, one morning I was trying to help out a scowling woman who had spent 30 minutes telling me, "I hate my job. The people are all straight."

the inflatable butch

I offered her *The Diplomatic Dyke: Twelve Tactful Tricks for Coming Out.*

"No," she said dully. "I'm sure they all know. But they don't want to deal with it, and neither do I."

I tried guiding her to our career section, then self-help, spirituality, even travel (sometimes it just helps to get away), but nothing pleased her.

"Maybe I just need a murder mystery," she finally said.

Maybe you need 12 months of analysis. "Of course. Third shelf to your right."

Other lost souls do know just what they want; they just don't know where to find it. A few months ago, a scruffy man in beat-up clothing wandered in and poked around anxiously. I assumed he was drunk, but, as he also could have been an eccentric humanities professor from the nearby university, I gave him full reign. Eventually, he made his way to the counter.

"Hi. Can I help you?"

"Yeah, I'm looking for those machines where you put in a quarter and peek inside."

"Ah," I said, maintaining full professionalism, "you want the adult bookstore." I aimed him out the door. "One block down on your left."

My all-time favorite customer was a young woman about 16 wearing black clothes, a rhinestone choker, and glasses with cat's-eye frames. She flipped through the vampire books, thumbed through the witchcraft section, mulled around the bulletin board.

the inflatable butch

Finally, she asked, "Do you have any books about...girlfriends?"

"You mean relationships?"

"No..."

"Sexuality?"

"No." She was getting frustrated. "I mean—how do you date girls? Boys are easy. They just want to do drugs and have sex." She sighed. "But girls—girls want to *talk* about everything."

And then there are those people who never make it into the store at all. Last week, after locking up for the night, I was a few yards from the store when two "professionals" from the architectural firm next door crossed my path.

"Hey," the well-groomed man said to his well-heeled friend, voice drenched in sarcasm, "wanna stop by the *lesbian* bookstore?"

I turned around and pasted on my biggest smile. "I'm sorry, sir," I said. "We're closed for the evening. But we open again at 10. Do stop by."

Ah, the mighty bookseller/barkeeper. She strikes another blow for freedom.

Mid-Life at Michigan

The Michigan Womyn's Music Festival. After years of postponing this lesbian rite of passage—it kept conflicting with book tours, family vacations, and uncooperative lovers—I decided to go for it. Alone.

Wanting to properly prepare for my adventure, I began to thoroughly and methodically pester my friends for information—what to bring, where to camp, what to expect. Unfortunately, this only confused matters. For instance, my friend Spider said, "Bring lots of clothes. Everything gets wet and dirty, and by the fourth day you'll be craving clean shirts and dry underwear." However, her girlfriend Louise advised, "Pack light. It's camping. The whole point is to get grimy." And these two have been together for ten years?

I also noticed a strange pattern to these informational sessions. No matter how they started, they

the inflatable
butch

always ended up on the same topic: sex.

"What kind of tent should I bring?" I asked, considering weight versus livability.

"A dome tent has the advantage of being more spacious," my friend Mage said, "allowing you to have a 'friend' visit without having her right on top of your sleeping bag. On the other hand, a pup tent has the advantage of allowing a friend to visit right on top of your sleeping bag." Chuckle, chuckle, wink, wink.

Discussions about just how many women would be there yielded the same results. "OK," my pals calculated, "you have roughly 6,000 women. Let's figure two thirds of them are unavailable right off the bat. That leaves 2,000. Now let's say that, for whatever reason, an entire 80% of them don't appeal to you—they're too boozy, too chatty, look too much like your last lover. Still, that leaves 400 women, or a potential 67 dates per day. That's 2.7 women per hour!"

To be honest, I wasn't going to Michigan to jump anyone's bones. But since I didn't want to crush my friends' vicarious fantasies, I played along. After two months, however, I was beginning to think having sex at Michigan was as much of a requirement as doing one's work shift. Hmm...maybe they were right—maybe a fling *would* make me feel desirable, hip, and vibrant.

August 10th found me disembarking from the festival bus, a week's worth of earthly belongings

the inflatable butch

jammed into my 22-year-old backpack. Feeling robust, I hiked the mile to Bush Gardens, on the lookout for wild young dykes. But the first dyke who confronted me was neither wild, young, or even neighborly. "Get off the road," she growled. "Use the path!"

Oh, my God, it's true, I thought. *Those stories about the humorless lesbian despots at Michigan.* I hadn't seen any path, didn't know the road was strictly for vehicles. Still, figuring that this "sister" was an unhappy drone during the rest of her life, I conjured up a few crumbs of compassion and left her alone to bask in her temporary tyranny. Locating the footpath, I trudged forward, on the lookout for more promising specimens of dykedom.

Soon, though, my attention turned from the search for curvaceous bodies to the search for level ground. Settling for a 10-degree slope, I began homesteading: setting up my tent, Therm-A-Rest, sleeping bag, and assorted clothes. Simple but neat, with plenty of room for a late-night guest—as long as she didn't mind a slight slant. Once again, I imagined a steamy night of flesh on flesh with an exuberant 20-year-old. Then I caught myself. Could I really sleep with someone younger than my backpack?

I trekked off to dinner but was stunned as I walked through the Over-50 area. This crowd didn't have campsites—they had complete subdivisions. Supplemented with patio furniture, clotheslines, prayer flags, and windsocks, their tents were the size

the inflatable butch

of my apartment, their rain tarps the span of Rhode Island. Suddenly, I was struck by a thunderbolt revelation: Who needed a youngster on the ground when I could have a gray-haired babe on a cot! Later, as I munched my lettuce-and-chickpea sandwich, I wondered, *Just when did lying on an air mattress become sexier than rolling around naked amongst the ferns?*

Later that evening I put the compulsory (or was that compulsive?) sex question aside and leafed through my festival guide, trying to transform the swirl of workshops, concerts, performances, and dances into something manageable. "Don't try to do everything," my friends had warned me, but I planned to anyway. As I manically flipped pages and made notes—day stage, night stage, intensive workshops, nonintensive workshops, films, drumming, readings—my proposed schedule made my regular workweek look dim by comparison. Should I get a massage? A haircut? Some holistic dental work? As dusk rolled in, I continued to study and memorize everything Michiganian—pedestrian pathways, concert-seating etiquette, proper use of the Porta-Janes.

Then it was off to my first formal event, the "Welcome Ritual and Drum Council." Stumbling down a narrow path, my bodhran in one hand, a flashlight in the other, I eventually found my way to a dimly lit clearing jammed with drummers, chanters, and watchers. It was hard to figure out what was going on, plus I'd missed the beginning,

which made me feel even more self-conscious. What did I, a white woman from trendy, vacuous Boulder, know about drumming? About ritual? About to give up and stumble back to my tent, I remembered Xena and Gabrielle! Imagining myself a brand of generic Amazon, I stayed and watched, tapping quietly on my drum and even offering a low-throated semi-rhythmic syllable or two. At least I didn't have to worry about the "finding a babe" question—it was too dark to see anyone.

Over the next five days, I experienced the variety-pack version of Michigan, also known as the lesbian-schizophrenia package. I took lots of workshops, such as Prepatriarchal Judaism and Mask-making (that's two workshops, not one, although at Michigan, it could have been one and nobody would have blinked twice). I also taught a workshop, Writing From Our Core. It wasn't about getting in touch with our inner rotten apple, but again, at Michigan it could have been—and been heartily attended at that.

I also watched several dyke films, marched in the giant puppet parade, won a craftswomon raffle (I didn't win a craftswomon herself, but instead her jewelry), traded at the barter tent (my books for necklaces, candles, and handmade deodorant), and heard Alice Walker read a smoldering sex scene in front of 2,000 enraptured lesbians. Early Saturday morning, I dragged myself out of my tent, pulled on my sneakers, chomped down a Power Bar, and made

the inflatable butch

my way to the 13th Annual Lois Lane Run, a one-mile fun run. Except it wasn't—it was actually a five-kilometer race and not all that fun. As I ran, walked, and limped along, I briefly considered disappearing into the Twilight Zone camping area, where I was sure loud and rowdy S/M dykes would offer me asylum until the race was long over and everyone forgot I was ever in it. But spurred on by cheering half-dressed women, I finished the race, bravely stumbling in third to last, beating out an amused racewalker and an eight-year-old girl. To celebrate my victory, I treated myself to a henna tattoo and a foot massage.

Somewhere in between all this I heard a lot of music—the Indigo Girls, Ferron, Sweet Honey In The Rock, Toshi Reagon, and a klezmer band. (No, Toshi didn't play with the klezmer band, but at Michigan she could have and no one...well, you know the story.)

So what happened to all the sex? Well, as I was camping out in line to get good seats for the Indigo Girls concert, I did have my bare back bodypainted by a 16-year-old. (Don't roll your eyes; her four friends and parental guardian were there at the time.) Actually, I was hoping to make the moves on her mother, a funny, well-muscled woman who brought her daughter to the festival each year. I was about to say something a bit more personal—something along the lines of "So how long have you been out?" or "Ever had tent sex?"—when she commented, "Isn't the festival wonderful? I always look forward

to getting a break from the house and my husband for a week."

Great. Six thousand lesbians at Michigan, and leave it to me to find the one straight woman. Forget licentious love and fervid flings, forget 2.7 women per hour—my days of random, tawdry sex are gone forever.

On the other hand, there's always next year.

```
POWELL'S CITY OF BOOKS
1005 WEST BURNSIDE
PORTLAND, OREGON  97209

503-228-4451        1-800-878-7323

QTY     PRODUCT          DEPT    PRICE
-------------------------------------
 1   MONTANA            317650    4.95
 1   HOW TO WRITE &     9E455056  7.50
 1   INFLATABLE BUTCH   250020    9.50
 1   SPACE CLEANSING    M493057   5.95

15477   TOTAL SALE              $27.90


   4    VISA                    $27.90
CARD NUMBER ************1544     01/07
DAGGETT/GINA N



** CUSTOMER COPY *** CUSTOMER COPY **

   00001 05-000 AJW  5/12/04  1:59 PM

PHOTO ID REQUIRED FOR ALL RETURNS.
MERCHANDISE MUST BE UNUSED AND BOOKS
UNREAD.  SEE REVERSE SIDE FOR FURTHER
RETURNS POLICY.
```

RETURNS POLICY

We accept returns within 14 days of purchase with your receipt. Your refund will correspond to the original form of payment. Books should be in the same condition as at time of sale.

Thank you for shopping at Powell's

POWELL'S CITY OF BOOKS
503 • 228 • 4651   800 • 878 • 7323

powells.com

Open 9am to 11pm every day

We buy & sell used books

RETURNS POLICY

We accept returns within 14 days of purchase with your receipt. Your refund will correspond to the original form of payment. Books should be in the same condition as at time of sale.

Thank you for shopping at Powell's

POWELL'S CITY OF BOOKS
503 • 228 • 4651   800 • 878 • 7323

powells.com

Open 9am to 11pm every day

We buy & sell used books

RETURNS POLICY

We accept returns within 14 days of purchase with your receipt. Your refund will correspond to the original form of payment. Books should be in the same condition as at time of sale.

Thank you for shopping at Powell's

POWELL'S CITY OF BOOKS
503 • 228 • 4651   800 • 878 • 7323

powells.com

Open 9am to 11pm every day

We buy & sell used books

RETURNS POLICY

Steaming

I was 16 years old when I bailed on Judaism. My Hebrew school rabbi was giving his lame "Women Aren't Lesser, Just Different" speech when I broke in, "But why do men get to make the rules in the first place?" After more hedging, he finally broke down. "Men," he told me, "are in charge because they initiate the sex act."

In response to *that* stunning display of logic, I spent the next 17 years hanging out with Buddhists, Quakers, and the occasional pagan. Only when Jewish Renewal moved into town did I dare venture back. Led by a smart woman rabbi, this version of Judaism intrigued me with its creative reclaiming of ritual, including an updated version of the *mikvah*. That's right, in Jewish Renewal you can score karma points for hot-tubbing.

Now, while Orthodox women go to male-rabbi-

the inflatable butch

blessed bathhouses, we Coloradans steam in the decidedly non-kosher caverns of Idaho Springs. Sounds like fun, huh? Except when reality steps in.

You see, this was my first year at the *mikvah*, and to make the unfamiliar even more bizarre, the night before I'd had a long "Are we friends or are we dating?" chat with a new pal. We decided to try dating for real, both agreeing to go slow—on the handholding, the kissing, the jumping into bed.

So flash-forward ten hours and here I am with my potential girlfriend and eight other women in the vapor caves, facing one another on slippery tile benches, all of us nude as fish. So much for slow.

Now, all this should be sexy, right? I am a lesbian, after all. But wait—I'm also a Jew, cleansing my soul for the New Year, plumbing my spiritual depths. Conflict! Conflict!

Actually, there is no conflict. Because even though, as a red-blooded dyke, I should be enjoying the view, I keep looking away from my naked, very new girlfriend, whose unclothed body I'm not supposed to be laying my eyes upon for months. Struggling with a mix of bashfulness and curiosity, I avert my eyes from her and look up to see—our rabbi!

Good Lord, this is even worse. One is not supposed to see one's rabbi—any rabbi—naked. It's blasphemous. What was I thinking—joining a group that welcomes lesbians?! I should have joined a bunch of fanatics who wouldn't have let me near them. Then I wouldn't be in a vapor cave with a

nude rabbi. To make it worse, our rabbi is one of those gorgeous straight women who works out.

Do any of the straight women feel uncomfortable? No. They're chatting away like dyke separatists, saying how good it is to disrobe, physically and psychically, in this women-only space (only they don't call it that). They have no qualms about sitting in the buff with a naked rabbi, a known lesbian (me), and her potential lover, who has great shoulder blades. OK, I peeked.

After the first immersion, I distract myself by imagining I'm at my Bat Mitzvah. But this time, as I belt out my *haftarah* portion, the whole congregation is sitting in a steaming vapor cave, naked. Yup, everyone is majorly el nudo, except for my grandmother, who of course wears her pearls, and my uncle, who never goes anywhere without his vest and handkerchief.

All this creative visualization helps me relax. I consider that, despite the comfortable chatter, others might also be pushing the edge of their comfort zones. It also dawns on me, after my second plunge, that rabbis, naked or clothed, are also human. Finally, I acknowledge that viewing my friend's unclothed bod won't force us to jump into bed. (Though it certainly isn't going to hurt.) Only one question remains: Has she been sneaking peeks at me?

I sure hope so.

What's My Dysfunction?

Hello and welcome to *What's My Dysfunction?*—the show that rewards bad boundaries with fabulous prizes. I'm your host, Sylvia Sloan. This week's theme, "Bad Boundaries With Ex-Lovers," drew entries from thousands of lesbians across the nation. From this unusually large field of candidates, we've whittled our finalists down to three.

With us now is our first contestant, Mavis Marsap. Five months ago, after swearing their eternal love for each other, Mavis and Georgia moved into an overpriced loft in a rapidly gentrifying part of town. Yet after only three weeks, Georgia left Mavis for Priscilla, a rich yet closeted WNBA star.

Stuck with a pricey lease, Mavis quickly depleted her savings. She then moved into a dumpy basement apartment, where, suffering from light deprivation,

the inflatable butch

she began exhibiting erratic behaviors such as building small-scale sculptures out of cockroaches and toothpaste. But that wasn't the worst of it, was it, Mavis?

Mavis: No, Sylvia. Six weeks after I moved into my apartment, my ex called to see if I'd house-sit for her and Patricia. They were off for vacation in Belize and needed someone to oversee the delivery and installation of their new hot tub.

Sylvia: You, of course, declined.

Mavis : Well, no. I agreed.

Sylvia: Audience?

Audience: Bad Boundaries!

Sylvia: But at least Georgia paid you generously for your house-sitting services?

Mavis: Actually, I paid them for the opportunity to—

Audience: Bad Boundaries! Bad Boundaries!

Sylvia: As our third-prize winner, Mavis, you'll receive three halogen lamps for your apartment, a tube of Crest, and a caller ID box. Screen those calls and stay away from your ex!

the inflatable butch

Our next contestant is Glenna Grumps. Glenna, tell us about your Bad Boundaries.

Glenna: [*ripping off her wig and sunglasses*] Ha! Fooled you, Sylvia! It's really me, Roz, your ex-lover from 1987. As a militant therapist infiltrator, I formally protest the degrading format of "Bad Boundaries." What are we going to hear next? "Honey, I'm throwing you out of my house, but would you pick me up an espresso on your way over to get your things?"

Sylvia: Thank you for those very clear sentiments, Roz—you haven't changed a bit. And as a thank-you for your participation, here's a lifetime subscription to *Contentious Dyke Quarterly*.

And now, for our next contestant, here's Josie Jefferson, an MCC minister. Josie, come on out here and tell us about your Bad Boundaries.

Josie: Well, Sylvia, I was with Teresa for eight years, after which we somewhat mutually split up. OK, OK—it wasn't mutual at all, but I didn't want Teresa to feel bad about herself, so I pretended to support her decision. Anyway, a year later Teresa and her new girlfriend, Delia, decided to get married. At first they didn't invite me, but then they realized they'd gone over-budget and needed someone to officiate for free. The thought of officiating made my stomach churn, but I didn't want to spoil her big day. So I said yes.

Audience: Baaaad Boundaries!

Josie: So as I stood in front of them and 200 assorted guests, I announced, "Teresa, when I told you ten years ago that I wanted to marry you, this isn't exactly what I had in mind."

Sylvia: Looks like you got the last laugh there, Josie! Not to mention today's first-place prize. Here's a $1,000 gift certificate toward six sessions with the therapist of your choice.

And that's it for today, friends. Please join us next week when our theme will be "Bad Boundaries With Our Cats." Until then, this is Sylvia Sloan saying, "Keep your walls up and your shades down!"

Putting the "Mary" Back in Merry Christmas

Exodus Ex-Gay Ministries, a group that has a better gay matchmaking track record than the top ten homo dating services combined, claims Jesus can "redeem" homosexuals. They even have a song about it (sung to the tune of "It's a Small World.")

> It's not in your genes, it's not in your brains!
> It's not chromosomes that cause you pain!
> Jesus Christ made a way!
> You don't have to be gay
> It's not inborn after all!

The stunningly sophisticated lyrics aside, I can't help wondering about Exodus's choice of Jesus as a model heterosexual.

the inflatable butch

Hetero? Does this sound like the life of a straight man? As a kid, Jesus is the victim of the absent father/overbearing mother syndrome. Oh, sure, Jesus's dad is omnipresent, but does he ever play ball with his son? Does he teach him to fish or change a tire or any of those father-son things so important to normal development? And while I have nothing but admiration for Mary, for the young Jesus, living under the shadow of a such a famous mom must have been awfully tough.

(Speaking of Mary—did she get a raw deal! A young homeless woman, mysteriously pregnant, she's forced to give birth in an abandoned building. Despite the odds, she bears not just a healthy baby boy, but the Son of God, for Pete's sake. After all that, you'd think they'd name the religion after *her*.)

Anyway, back to the kid. As a teenager, Jesus is the perfect son, typical of young gay men trying to prove themselves. As a carpenter, he's but a few steps away from a career in interior design. But instead Jesus embarks on a desert vision quest, getting baptized by his cousin John and basically going on to become a long-haired, Birkenstock-wearing, establishment-challenging, big ol' radical faerie.

We all know that Jesus hung out with 12 disciples, didn't marry, didn't have kids. We know that among his original followers, John was the "one he loved most." We know of the drama queen nature of the apostles' bickering, betrayals, and jealousy. And of course, we know that Mary Magdalene was a major fag hag.

ellen orleans

But also consider if anyone is obsessed with dinner parties, it's a gay man. So, who turned water into wine? Jesus did. Who turned a paltry number of fish and loaves into a meal for the masses? Jesus did. The man really knew how to celebrate with food and drink—why, his last supper was such a feast that he even had Leonardo da Vinci paint it. Without a doubt, here's a man, celibate or not, who lived the homosexual lifestyle.

However, so you know I hold no hard feelings toward all you folks at Exodus, let me be the first to send my season's greetings: a Fairy Mary Christmas to all!

Toys Aren't Us

Last June, I spent an evening in Greenwich Village, where the queers are so hip, I have no idea what they're talking about. For instance, in one shop, I picked up a flyer that proclaimed "Gay Shame '99!" OK, I got that, big irony and all. But by the second line—vegan potluck and tabling at 5 P.M., Red Monkey at 7 P.M.—I was completely lost. What is tabling? Is it related to lap dancing—which hasn't been cutting edge since '95 and still I've never seen it in action? And what is Red Monkey? A mixed drink? A transgender spanking game? Do I even want to know?

So here I am at an outdoor café, sitting with M.J., a longtime pal from high school days—and Davi, a dyke author I've just met. I'm whining to both of them about how removed I feel from the queer avant-garde, when suddenly I look down the

street and notice the Pleasure Chest, the Village's infamous sex-toy shop. Good-bye, naïveté! Hello, brush with bad girl!

I persuade them to come with me, and together we wander in, past the chocolate penis lollipops and candy breasts. The store is small but well-lit, populated by men and women, both gay and straight, in a variety of colors and ages, casually chatting and browsing. Looking around, I see harnesses and dildos, blow-up dolls and handcuffs, plus a stack of Hitachis, the standard-issue lesbian vibrator. I try to tune in to the nervy, bad-girl energy, but I can't. The place is about as wild as a Hallmark shop. I sigh.

Still, as long as I'm here, I might as well check out the merchandise. Who knows, maybe I'll find a Red Monkey. So M.J., Davi, and I wander around, more puzzled than aroused. On the far wall, there's the Silicon Milkmaid—"Please touch and suck my huge breasts," her packaging reads.

"Now, that's titillating," remarks M.J. while stifling a yawn. She writes promotional copy for a living and is, therefore, particular. She turns to another item on the shelf. "*Juli Ashton's ULTRAREALISTIC Tits and Ass.*" An ordinary white girl adorns the box cover; she lies on her stomach, her supposedly exciting butt exposed to all.

"Can you imagine being the design person for this?" M.J. asks. "Let's see, our pullout copy will be 'ULTRAREALISTIC'—all caps, italic text. No,

the inflatable butch

wait. Maybe we should emphasize 'Tits and Ass' and triple the point size."

Several items we find downright confusing. The first is a rubber cock attached to an oversize ball. What is this for—erotic kickball, lewd volleyball? Or is it a twist on those exercise fitness balls: Give your quadriceps a workout while bouncing your way to orgasm?

Next there's "The Ultrarealistic Male: Firm Cock and Tight Ass." It's a packaged set. We are quite perplexed by this one. I mean, who exactly is their target audience? A straight couple? No, she has his cock and he has her ass. A gay male couple? It's redundant. A lesbian couple? No, the ass is superfluous. Unless one of them wants to strap on the dildo and pump plastic while the other one watches. Maybe *that's* doing the "Red Monkey."

Our last stop is the dildo section, which sports a colorful array of products in many shapes and sizes. Looking them over, I finally get up my nerve and ask, "What exactly is the average size of a penis?" I figure every modern woman, hetero or not, should know this. And since the only penises I've seen belong to six-month-old sons of my lesbian friends or to gay male porn stars whose videos I've watched with my queeny pals, I don't have a realistic vision. I point to a bright blue dildo with pink veins. "Is this average?"

Davi laughs. "If you're a horse."

M.J., who's dipped her toes in both ends of the

ellen orleans 143

dating pool, points to a cinnamon-colored dildo that looks not unlike a substandard hot dog. "Now, there's your average wiener," she says.

Is she joking? Is Davi? I decide not to pursue the matter, although I can't help wondering, glancing back at Dildo Jr., *Red Monkey?*

We leave the Pleasure Chest without treasures, pleasures, or chests other than our own. Finding another café, we indulge instead in conversation, cups of upscale decaf, and a shared slice of real New York cheesecake.

The Red Monkey, seated on her cryptic table, will have to wait till next time.

Multiple-Choice Madness

Faced with recent and medically confirmed mid-life crisis, I realized I had only three possible choices in life:

1. have a baby.
2. become a Buddhist nun.
3. go to graduate school.

Acknowledging that I have a short attention span, I promptly eliminated options one and two. Left with choice three, I got on the Web and began ferreting out graduate school home pages. I quickly learned all I must do to apply—fill out forms, write essays, obtain transcripts, and...take the GRE.

No sweat, I thought. *I'll just buy a prep book, memorize a few algebraic constructs, a handful of*

the inflatable butch

geometric formulas. I did it my senior year of college; I can do it 16 years later.

Yeah, right.

I tried. Honestly, I did. But forget the math, I couldn't get past the social implications of the word problems. I have no idea why, but my answers just did not match up.

Question:

If four cows produce four cans of milk in four days, how many days does it take eight cows to produce eight cans of milk?

Answer:

I'm lactose-intolerant. Next question.

Question:

At the office, Ann, Bill, Carol, Don, and Ed work in five cubicles lined up against a wall. Only the last cubicle has a window. Arrange their seating to satisfy the following conditions.

Carol cannot sit next to Don, who smokes.

Ann talks loudly on the phone and cannot sit next to Bill, who needs quiet.

Ed's employment contract stipulates a window in his cubicle area.

Answer:

First, instigate a no-smoking rule. That takes care of Don's little problem. Next, tear down those

the inflatable butch

stupid cubicles and build real offices with doors that shut. While you're at it, punch in some holes for windows. Everyone happy?

Actually, the real problem is this: Who cares about white-bread Ann, Bill, Carol, Don, and Ed? The GRE creators have told me nothing about their personal struggles or spiritual paths or even what they're all doing in those cubes. Are they fund-raisers for liberal causes or merely pushy telemarketers? This matters to me. But since the authors of the GRE never tell us, I have no empathy for the five of them—and consequently, little motivation to solve their problem. Frankly, I'm not an office manager, nor am I going to graduate school to become one.

As I see it, it's time to update the GRE, give it a postmodern queer twist. Yup, it's time for the Gay Reality Examination—an exam we can relate to. So grab your No. 2 pencils, everyone, and remember: On this test, creativity counts!

Question #1

Part 1

Dr. Hannah Helpsome sees five regular clients on Tuesday afternoons: Anjali, Becky, Calvin, Delores, and Ernie. Her sessions begin on the hour and last 55 minutes. Using the criteria below, in what order must Hannah schedule these five clients if her time slots are 1, 2, 3, 4, and 5 P.M.?

the inflatable butch

Becky is the last radical lesbian separatist in town and will spend 15 minutes fuming if she runs into a male in Hannah's waiting room.

Delores's blood sugar tends to get low after 4 P.M., making her temporarily distracted and depressed.

On alternate Tuesdays, Anjali has aromatherapy until 1:30 and gravity inversion therapy from 3:30 to 4:30.

Ernie's MTF transgender discussion group meets from noon to 1:30 P.M. each week.

Calvin, a bisexual activist, wishes to avoid both Becky and Ernie, recent ex-lovers.

Part 2
Once Ernie self-defines as female, is Hannah ethically able to see lesbian separatist Becky at 4 P.M.?
 a. Yes, since not to do so would set back Ernie's progress three months.
 b. No, she must honor Becky's, not Ernie's, definition of gender identity.
 c. Doesn't matter because Becky is about to tell her that she and Ernie had sex over the weekend.

Part 3
If Anjali drops aromatherapy and instead undergoes vibrational tuning-fork healing from 10

to 11, can Hannah then see Anjali at 1 P.M.?
- a. Yes, if Anjali's ears have stopped ringing.
- b. No, Calvin would have a fit it he lost his 1 o'clock slot.
- c. No, Hannah must drop Anjali as Hannah holds stock in the Harmonic-BioSonic Tuning Fork Company.

Part 4

Isn't Hannah overdoing it, seeing five clients in a row?
- a. Yes, and she must come to terms with her workaholic-savior tendencies.
- b. No, what with HMOs and insurance limitations, she's smart to pack 'em in whenever she gets the chance.
- c. Doesn't matter, as her office building is about to be torn down and turned into a Starbucks.

How's That Again?

Just when you thought your anatomy was safe from scrutiny, we're hit with headlines from yet another whacked-out research experiment, "Study: Gays Have Short Index Fingers." Except I have a long index finger. Guess I'll have to turn in my lesbian ID.

All this reminds me of another study a few years back: "Scientific Breakthrough: Lesbians' Inner Ear Different." Lesbian inner ears, gay index fingers, the homo hypothalamus—what's next, bisexual kneecaps? Transgender eyebrows? "Yup, Velma, just look at that boy's eyebrows. He'll be wearing pumps and hose by the time he's 12, mark my words."

Where will this end? Lesbian armpits: .03% more hair follicles. Gay male toenails: two shades pinker than hetero nails (and cleaner too).

But back to our ears. According to the Associated Press, it's the lesbian "cochlea" that's making news.

the inflatable butch

(And here I was all these years, thinking *cochlea* was Yiddish for *tiny penis*. Who knew?)

Anyway, apparently lesbians' cochleae (that's plural for *cochlea*, the sound amplifier in the inner ear) behave more like men's. Researchers at the University of Texas said our cochleae have undergone "masculinization," probably from "hormone exposure before birth." (You can now thank your mother for making you gay. Literally.)

But the phrase that struck me here was "masculinization of the cochlea." What does this mean? That my cochlea has a sense of entitlement? That it's always right? That it takes up more than its fair share of space on park benches?

In this case, apparently, the effect of masculinization is that our hearing is less sensitive than that of het women's, with men's cochlea yet weaker. Bisexuals are (once again) in the middle. I, however, find it no surprise that lesbian hearing is less sensitive. After all, who wants to hear what people say to us?

"Ya fuckin' lesbo!"

"Lousy dyke commie!"

"Faggot!" (This one always confuses me.)

"Hey, baby, you wanna see what a real man looks like?" (He then whips out his cochlea.)

And what's up with the test group in this study? "The sexual orientation of the subjects was determined by questionnaire." Questionnaire? We all know how scientific self-definition is. Did they have check boxes for:

ellen orleans

[ ] lesbians who sleep with gay men for political reasons;

[ ] lesbians who sleep with men for no particular reason;

[ ] heterosexual, married women who've been having sex with the neighbor lady for 30 years?

More to the point, have the researchers differentiated sensitivity levels for stone butches, high femmes, blazer dykes, and postmodern queer grrls? Let's not even get into gender expression.

Still, there must be an evolutionary basis for this—although biology does seem backwards here. Imagine a hulking Neanderthal—no, not your supervisor at work; I mean a real prehistoric Neanderthal guy crouched down on the savanna. Amid the squawking of ornithosaurs and the scampering of herbivorous reptiles, he'd have to listen closely for the rustling of tall grasses telling him prey is near. Wouldn't this guy need sensitive, not dulled, hearing? Then again, if it were a two-ton mammoth he was stalking—STOMP!! STOMP!! Squash!—after a few centuries, the need for acute hearing probably just dwindled away.

Conversely, imagine the Neanderthal straight woman, stuck at home with six screaming near-ape kids, packs of crazed mastodons thundering past her cave door—why in the world would anyone need to hear all that any more loudly than necessary? But I guess she had to be alert for the menfolks' return, so

she'd have plenty of time to stoke the fire for the mammoth-burgers.

Lesbian Neanderthals, on the other hand, weren't having sex with men and hence weren't having bucketloads of children. Instead, deep in the hush of subterranean caverns, they munched happily on marsh ferns and whortleberries as they painted intricate murals on the cave walls. And you can imagine what a few millennia of peace and quiet can do to developing inner ears...

Back in this century, though, I can feel this study's ramifications already. At the gates of the Michigan Womyn's Music Festival, lesbian sentries will be whipping out their Q-Tips and otoscopes, checking out each woman's cochlean credentials as she files on in.

Hmm...guess it beats counting armpit follicles.

All Tied Up

As a lesbian writer, I get a lot of queer junk mail, but the following promotion beat the competition hands down. It started with a full-color brochure:

You've been hearing about it for years, reading about it in books, watching allusions to it in those upscale noir films. Heck, you've even been known to sport cuffs and chains at more than one Halloween party. Yet the fact remains: You've never actually tried S/M.

Don't worry, you're not alone. That's right, just like you, thousands of lesbian Americans have been afraid—because of misinformation, internalized oppression, boring sex partners, or bad accessories— to venture into the glamorous world of S/M. But fret no longer because we've got the perfect introductory

the inflatable butch

workshop for you: S/M Lite! Just pop in the enclosed video to hear all about it.

Hastily canceling my afternoon appointments, I parked myself in front of my VCR and slid in the cassette. A bouncy bright-eyed lesbian filled the screen:

Hi! I'm Cheryl. Want to know if S/M is for you—before investing in expensive dildo harnesses and hand-tooled whips? With our low-cost, no-pressure weekend workshop, it's easy! That's right, you'll learn the ins and outs of basic S/M, work through your socially induced prejudices, and most importantly, figure out whether you're a top or a bottom.

At S/M Lite (Cheryl continued) our seminar leaders are professionals whose decades of S/M experience have included dozens of partners. In fact, odds are at least one of our instructors has had sex with your girlfriend!

Our innovative, hands-on classes include:

• Knot Tying 101: Not Just for Girl Scouts Anymore.

• Shoe Polish on the Dildo: Common Mistakes Beginners Make.

• Hot Wax! Produce Painful Pleasure While Removing Unsightly Pubic Hair Forever.

• Cyber-Sex: Is She Faking It?

• And many more!

For you literary gals, we offer several workshops featuring such writers as Agony Elmgrove, author of

the inflatable butch

the touching S/M romance series *Love, Leather, and Lubrication*; Pat Titclampia, editor of the 1998 anthology *Love Me Till It Hurts*; and Susie Dull, whose book *Sexual State of Confusion* recently won the coveted Golden Showers award.

After your workshops, be sure to drop by our gift shop, which features the latest in sex-toy technology. Got a butchy fix-it-upper on your shopping list? Surprise her with the two-in-one vibrator/power drill kit. That's right, the drill bits are stored right inside for that "do me now, drill the holes for the eye screws later" convenience.

Got a pea-size bladder? Treat yourself to our dual-action vibrator/flashlight. Twist to the right for God-inducing orgasms, to the left for a powerful beam of light to guide you to the bathroom or refrigerator or even the front door. Great for one-night stands in strange apartments.

For you earthier types, try out our organic edible underwear, made from pesticide-free soybeans, or our "Save the Earth" butt plugs, made from recycled pop bottles. Because, at S/M Lite, we know that environmentally friendly orgasms are the best!

Does S/M Lite sound too good to be true? Don't take our word for it. Listen to what our satisfied participants have to say:

(The video then showed a group of sweet-faced lesbian-next-door types who each confessed in turn.)

"I admit it. I had some big hang-ups about bondage. That is, until my group facilitator, Brenda,

helped demystify the process. Now I see that being tied up isn't so different from being immobilized by my lover's golden retriever lying across on my feet, something I got used to a long time ago. Now I'm having hotter sex than ever! Thanks, Brenda!"

"I used to think I was too busy for S/M sex, what with all those household chores eating up our weekends. Now that I've made scrubbing the bathroom and changing the litter box part of my lover's 'slave' duties, we've got plenty of time for fooling around!"

"My gal's an outside-the-house type: watering the lawn, washing the car, cleaning the gutters. I could never get her inside for sex. But once S/M Lite showed me how to include a garden hose in our lovemaking, my girlfriend's keeping *me* wet 24 hours a day!"

(Cheery Cheryl returned to the screen.)

"Have bigger orgasms sooner by registering for our July 1st weekend now. Just call the 800 number at the bottom of your screen."

July 1st? Let's see—appointment with a Broadway director, meeting with a New York publisher, second interview with a grant committee.

Clearly, I had my priorities. Picking up the phone, I dialed 1-800-Do-It-To-Me-Baby. To heck with the literary world: It was time to learn the ropes.

And the chains.

Poly-Parade Fidelity

I admit it: I'm a pride parade slut.

Each June, instead of committing to and marching with a single group, I find a cool spot on a curb and watch the queers stride by. At some point, when a good-looking group appears, I leap in, walking with them until I get bored. Then I jump ship, waiting on the sidelines for the next attractive entourage.

While I acknowledge my intimacy issues (unable to commit to a single organization), I don't march in the parade with just anyone. I must share common interests with them, I must feel that deep sense of connection. For instance, I've marched with the men and women of MCC (I've attended services there), AT&T (I own a phone), and PFLAG (I have parents).

This year, I entered the parade when the Denver

the inflatable butch

Public Library gay employee group came along. Once again, my participation was justifiable, since I read books. After nine blocks (and countless wolf whistles aimed at the librarians), I expressed my gratitude and peeled off.

Leaning against a parking sign, I continued to watch. The participants were mostly bar groups, church groups, or Fortune 500 employee groups. Gone were the witty handmade signs and left-wing politics. In their place, rainbow flags. Is this what happens when our marches are sponsored by Coors Lite—we get Parade Lite?

But then, near the end of the parade, Boulder appeared. My homies! The Boulder group was led by none other than Colorado's bare-breasted Lesbian Avengers. Just what I needed to get my juices flowing. I quickly fell in step, enjoying their anarchy, enjoying the view. I walked with Boulder for four blocks, eight blocks, 12 blocks! And still, I stayed with them. I was making a parade commitment!

Then I knew I must take my commitment one step further. Inspired by the rowdy, shirtless women before me (chanting "Take off your shirt! Take off your shirt!"), I decided that I—yes, Ellen Orleans, white girl from the suburbs of New Jersey—wanted to experience toplessness. I wanted to feel the breeze against my chest. I wanted to make a political statement.

Theoretically, at least.

I spent the next block debating it. And the next

the inflatable

butch

one and the next. Could I get up my nerve? Could I really do it? I was wearing two tank tops, a snug one under a loose one. I started by taking off the loose one. I marched one block like that. My friend Lili, next to whom I was walking, preferred to remain fully clothed herself, but encouraged me to bare all. "You're a writer," she said. "Do it for the sake of your art."

We drew ever closer to the end of the route. It was now or never. The Avengers continued to chant, "Take off your shirt!"

I did. People cheered. (Now, I've taken my shirt off in front of lovers, nurses, and women in locker rooms. But no one ever cheered before. Cool.)

So what happened? Did I raise my arms in a power salute as I marched along? Did I feel fearless and empowered? Robust, wild, and free? No, no, and no. So what did I feel? Frankly, I felt exposed. Exposed and...well, pale.

Holding my UNAFFILIATED DYKES OF BOULDER sign in front of me, I positioned myself between two bare-breasted Avengers. And not for the stimulation either—just to blend in better. Yep, I was sure that my parents, my eighth-grade English teacher, every former lover, and probably my childhood rabbi were all standing just one block ahead, ready to shake their heads in sad disbelief.

I made it three and a half blocks before I put my shirt back on.

Not exactly the defiant act I'd imagined, but a

start. And who knows, maybe next year I'll go topless again. And maybe, just maybe, next year I'll last a whole 12 blocks.

What a commitment.